# Mary Lou Carney

# SPIRITUAL HARVEST

Reflections on the Fruit of the Spirit

ABINGDON PRESS

NASHVILLE

SPIRITUAL HARVEST: REFLECTIONS ON THE FRUIT OF THE SPIRIT

*Copyright © 1987 by Abingdon Press*

This book is printed on acid-free paper.

**Library of Congress Cataloging-in-Publication Data**
CARNEY, MARY LOU, 1949-
   Spiritual harvest.
   1. Fruit of the Spirit. I. Title.
BV4501.2.C3165        1987        234'.13        87-1793

**ISBN 0-687-39231-4 (pbk.: alk. paper)**

All Scripture quotations, unless otherwise noted, are from the Holy Bible, New International Version. Copyright © 1973 by the New York Bible Society. Used by permission.

All Scripture quotations noted RSV are from the Revised Standard Version of the Bible, copyrighted 1946, 1952, © 1971, 1973 by the Division of Christian Education of the National Council of the Churches of Christ in the U.S.A., and are used by permission.

All Scripture quotations noted TLB are from *The Living Bible,* copyright © 1971 by Tyndale House Publishers, Wheaton, Ill. Used by permission.

All Scripture quotations noted KJV are from the King James Version of the Bible.

Facts for hymn backgrounds are taken from the following:
   *HYMN STORIES FOR PROGRAMS,* by Ernest K. Emurian; Baker Book House; Grand Rapids, Michigan; 1963. Used by permission.
   *FAMOUS STORIES OF INSPIRING HYMNS,* by Ernest K. Emurian; Baker Book House; Grand Rapids, Michigan 1956. Used by permission.

MANUFACTURED BY THE PARTHENON PRESS AT
NASHVILLE, TENNESSEE, UNITED STATES OF AMERICA

for

---

*BILL* and *LINDA CROWLEY*

---

m y

*fruitful friends*

# CONTENTS

# INTRODUCTION

---

*The fruit of the Spirit is love, joy, peace, patience, kindness, goodness, faithfulness, gentleness and self-control.*

Galatians 5:22

MOTHER AND I WERE SITTING IN THE YARD ONE SUNDAY afternoon when a stranger's car pulled into our driveway. It was the biggest, blackest automobile I had ever seen. Two men in suits sat in front, and in the back were two ladies with red lips and colorful, tilted hats. City folk. We walked over to the car and the windows slid down all by themselves, slick as butter on a hot biscuit.

A curly-haired lady leaned out the rear window. She had hair the color of ripe wheat and reminded me of a Kewpie doll at the state fair. "Sorry to bother you," she began, "but we are just so-o-o-o impressed with your flower gardens. Why, those geraniums are bigger than coffee cups, and I've never seen petunias so profuse!" The other lady kept nodding her head and smiling. "I'm quite a gardener myself," the Kewpie doll went on, "but my flowers couldn't hold a candle to yours. What *is* your secret?" She looked up at us through long curly lashes and smiled.

Without batting an eye mother replied, "Manure."

The lady's smile faded a touch. "Umm . . . you mean fertilizer?"

"No," Mother said stoically. "I mean manure."

"Oh." She looked even more like a Kewpie doll with her

mouth poised in a perfect "O." "Well . . . thank you, I'm sure."

The window slithered up; the fancy car backed out of our drive and was soon out of sight on the dusty road.

Manure. The very "earthiness" of this answer had made it unattractive. Sometimes we Christians are like that city lady. We are eager to heed Christ's command to "bear much fruit" (John 15:8). But we would become fruitful by philosophizing or serving on committees or donating to charities or reading spiritual bestsellers. But to be fruitful is to do more than these. It is to be fertilized by lowly, lusterless labors. It is to know discipline and determination and surrender of self.

*Spiritual Harvest* takes a fresh and practical look at the fruit of the Spirit—through scripture and biblical example, through personal illustration and insight, and through backgrounds for some of the great hymns of the church. *Spiritual Harvest* emphasizes the fact that bearing fruit is not a Christian option; it is the direct and sure result of the Holy Spirit's indwelling. Just as a master gardener tills his crop to rid it of weeds and worms, so God cultivates and prunes us. His tools are the opportunities and frustrations of daily living, the trivia and trials that make us send our roots deep into his resources.

It is my hope that this book will put you in touch with the realities of love, joy, peace, patience, kindness, goodness, faithfulness, gentleness, and self-control in your own life. It is my prayer that you will determine anew to bear fruit for the Lord.

And that it will be an abundant harvest.

*SPIRITUAL HARVEST*

## CHAPTER ONE

---

*Love is not blind—it sees more, not less. But because
it sees more, it is willing to see less.*

Rabbi Julius Gordon

## L O V E

---

LOVE. YOU HEAR THE WORD EVERY TIME YOU TURN ON
the radio. Bands blare it, and sensual voices sing it. It
seems to be the one commodity everyone is searching for,
the magical solution to every problem, from loneliness to
acne. Love.

Advertisements entice us with their promise of "You'll
love it!" Everything from creme-filled donuts to Carib-
bean cruises makes the same claim:"You'll *love* it!" We
are bombarded by the imperative to love, as though love
were something to be oozed like lava from an active
volcano.

But it isn't that simple. The songwriters forget to
mention that sometimes love is difficult; sometimes it's
lonely; often it is less than exhilarating. The advertisers
hawk their products, forgetting that love is not something
lavished on inanimate things, such as dishwashing liquid
or carpet deodorizer. Love is not granted on a whim; it is
not conferred with predictable patterns.

Every February, as Valentine's Day approaches, the
commercialization of love moves into full swing. Store
windows literally burst with huge red hearts and just the
right item to purchase for that special someone. Card
shops boast row upon row of wishes to celebrate the
occasion. Every sentiment, from romantic to raw, sprawls

*13*

in shades of pink and scarlet. Flower shops take out larger ads in the local newspapers—and raise the price of roses by twenty percent. The ancients believed that the most delicate of nerves ran from the third finger on the left hand directly to the heart. Thus the custom was initiated of wearing engagement and wedding rings on that finger. Perhaps the sense of anatomy was erroneous, but the sentiment is one to be considered seriously. To a heart that loves, the hands are the avenue of expression for that love, not only in caressing and carrying expensive gifts, but more aptly in service and deeds of devotion as well.

Read again I Corinthians 13, the great love chapter of the Bible. Even a quick perusal of this passage clarifies any confusion between love and lust. Lust is self-serving; love is selfless. Lust is temporal; love is eternal.

But the standards of love set forth in this chapter seem to border on the impossible. When your child has spilled his third glass of milk at dinner, your smiling a loving, patient smile does not come naturally. When your neighbor's dog has ruined your freshly planted flower bed, honest anger may be your immediate response. And who can "keep no record" of the wrongs committed by a jealous colleague, a spiteful neighbor, or a hypocritical "friend"? Then comes that formidable string of all-inclusive *always:* love *always* protects, *always* trusts, *always* hopes, *always* perseveres. Always?

"Impossible!" you groan.

It is impossible, in our own strength. The basic human impulses are toward "me first" tendencies. Yet the very core of love is indiscriminate selflessness. Love is not something we decide to wear one morning, like gold earrings or red shoes. It is, rather, a natural outgrowth of an inner state. It is not a response to human overtures or catchy clichés. It is an outward sign of a spiritual state of well-being. Externals reflect internals. Always.

True love is sincere, devout, selfless, and forgiving. It is humble and hospitable, constant and overcoming. It demonstrates itself not in wild spurts of passion or passing allegiance, but in service. Love is faith given feet and hands—and smiles. Galatians 5:6 reminds us that "the only thing that counts is faith expressing itself through love." Love is the expression of a forgiven heart, a heart so awed at being loved by God that it can do no less than love others.

The love of God is both our example and our inspiration. Isaiah 65:24 shows us the magnanimity of God's love: "Before they call I will answer." When I was a child, I was a very sound sleeper. Thunder storms, clanging alarm clocks, ringing telephones—nothing could wake me. But after I became a parent, the slightest cry or sound from my children brought me wide awake. Often I would wake to a silent house, but with a sense of urgency. Checking on the children, I would find one shivering on the edge of the bed, his covers kicked onto the floor, or maybe a soaked diaper was forcing him awake, or he was struggling with a stuffy nose. I had been awakened to care for these needs, awakened by a bond of love so strong it bordered on the intuitive. God's love for us is like that—strong, parental, absolute—and that fact gives us the courage and the power to love others.

Perhaps no scripture presents this parental love of God more clearly than Zephaniah 3:17:

> The Lord your God is with you,
>   he is mighty to save.
> He will take great delight in you,
>   he will quiet you with his love,
>   he will rejoice over you with singing.

When we had our first child, I was the prototype of a nervous new parent. I read all the books. I attended parenting classes. I bit my nails. But it didn't take me long to realize that my baby would often cry for no apparent reason—she was dry; she was fed; she was warm; she was well—but still she would cry. So I began to do something the books and classes hadn't told me, something my heart told me, instead. Whenever she was fussy and continued to cry, I would pick her up, hold her close, and love her, really love her. And as we rocked, I hummed a nameless tune that welled up inside while we snuggled in that cocoon of love. Soon she became still, quieted—literally—with my love.

God does this for us, his children, too. In our frenzy of service and complaint, in our rush of routine and role-playing, he takes us in his arms and saturates us with his love. Then he places us back into the tedium of life so we can love others as he has loved us. Our strategy for those annoying, grating peole we meet is not confrontation; it is love. We are to quiet them with what Paul calls "the most excellent way."

God gives his love unconditionally. When we least deserve it, his love is most insistent. The prophet Joel admonishes us, when we have strayed, to avail ourselves of this love.

> Return to the Lord your God,
>   for he is gracious and compassionate,
> slow to anger and abounding in love.
>                                   Joel 2:13

The department store was crowded with "Dollar Day" shoppers. Everything from cheese graters to gas grills was on sale. A clerk walked past me, his arms loaded with newly arrived teddy bears. In a flash, my three-year-old jerked her hand from mine and disappeared into the crowd, trailing the stuffed menagerie.

I tried to follow her, bumping and jostling my way through the throng, calling my daughter's name and mumbling apologies to women whose feet I was trampling. But soon salesman and teddy bears and toddler had all disappeared. I went from aisle to aisle, my heart beating in my ears, my voice coarse from yelling my daughter's name.

I did, finally, find her. Close to tears, she was sitting in the manager's office. "Mommy! Mommy!" she squealed, running into my open arms.

Was I angry with her for running from me, for not coming when I called? Perhaps. But when I remember that incident, the emotion I recall is love, pure, simple, complete. The lost had been found. All was well.

God calls us, through the fruit of the Holy Spirit, to offer that forgiving love, not just to our children and loved ones, but to those who least deserve it, to those who crush us and test us, to those who annoy us with their cynicism and sarcasm. If we would bear the fruit of love, we must let God's love bind us to him in adoration, devotion, and service. We must make his love our example of love bestowed consistently for Christ's sake. Then we must go and do likewise.

In Romans 5:8, Paul tells us that "God demonstrates his own love for us in this: While we were still sinners, Christ died for us." God's love is not a lofty, remote theory; it is a concrete reality. It is the suffering of innocence for my guilt, his death for my life. Love demands demonstration.

We heard it late one night on our local Christian radio station: My ten-year-old son Brett was busy building a city out of blocks, and I was getting an early start on wrapping Christmas presents. An international organization was soliciting gifts for the orphans of Central America. They were urging American children to take an empty shoe box and fill it with small presents and personal items for a homeless child. Brett and I both stopped working and listened. Hurriedly I copied the address while Brett headed out to the garage for just the right shoe box, one with a long-eared, sad-eyed dog on its lid. What fun we had packing that box! Brett chose carefully—a yo-yo, bubbles, a new toothbrush, soap, drawing paper and markers, hard candy, a small wooden cross, and a Spanish New Testament. He labored over each decision, imagining, as the announcer had suggested, that the only possessions the child might have would be what he or she received in that shoe box. Finally, Brett tucked in his school picture and return address. Then we wrapped and mailed the box.

But we didn't forget about it. All through the Christmas season we thought about that shoe box, wondering who would receive it, imagining his or her face as each treasure was lifted from its tissue paper. That gift of love filled our holiday with special meaning, with the freshness of giving with no hope of remuneration. This small act of giving had made real our love and concern for the tragic victims of Central America's poverty and political unrest.

Then, at the end of January, a letter arrived from Costa Rica. Its return address was stamped "Home for Orphans." Inside was a letter from Estaban, thanking his friend Brett for the gifts and wishing us all a happy new year. If we can just remember the lesson of the shoe box, the lesson of demonstrated love, it will, indeed, be a happy year.

Real love is not dependent on conditions; it is not an emotion of convenience. God's accusation against his people is that their love is temporary: "Your love is like the morning mist, like the early dew that disappears" (Hosea 6:4).

I have always had an aversion to spiders. If I see one

wiggle its way up the wall, my skin seems to prickle for hours. Even as a child, I could be coaxed near a web on only one condition.

Each day I would take the garden path to the chicken coop, where I would gather whatever eggs our reluctant hens had laid. Between the rows of corn stretched huge spider webs, weighted with morning dew. Shafts of sun fell on these droplets, creating tiny imprisoned rainbows. I was fascinated, and often I mustered the courage to inspect the wonder of this crystalline web close at hand.

But by noon, the dew droplets were gone. The web had taken on a cold, metallic look, and inevitably a huge yellow-and-black spider glared out from its middle.

Morning dew—few things are as beautiful or as fleeting. God's admonition to us is plain. Our love is not to be the fleeting, ornamental kind. It is, rather, to be deep and eternal, based on the knowledge that God himself is love. He always has loved; he always will love. And we, his children—created in his image, adopted into his family, filled with his Holy Spirit—are called to do the same. If we attempt to love in our own strength, we will find our love temporal, indecisive, and weak. But with God's help, our love can be eternal, unwavering, and strong. The fruit of the Holy Spirit is a love that grows and upholds, one that stands the storms of circumstance. Daily his Spirit will give us a renewed vision of God's love, so that we can, in turn, give it to others.

Today many Christians are caught in the trap of self-criticism and self-abasement. We never do enough for the Lord; we are never really *good* enough. Our drive to be the perfect Christian not only paralyzes our ministry, but it also makes us critical and unforgiving toward the inevitable flaws of others. In John 15:12, Jesus tells us, "My command is this: Love each other as I have loved you."

The first game of the Little League season is always a tense one. Fireflies flicker in the outfield as the teams warm up, eyeing each other with false bravado. There is the flip of a coin, and the game begins. Mitts hang from the hands of bantam basemen; chatter drifts through the popcorn-scented dusk. A crack of the bat, and bleachers reel with the screams of excited parents. Innings pass with homeruns and strikeouts, with overthrows and fumbled flies. But when the last puff of dust has settled and the scoreboard has recorded the final numbers, my son's coach always does the same things. He gives each would-be star a cold soda, a bit of advice, and a quick, hard hug. Throughout the summer those boys grow, basking in Coach's tough but unconditional love.

God's love is like that, too. Tough. Unconditional. We, as Christians, must accept our fallibility, and the fallibility of our fellow creatures. We must have the faith to expect God's love, to feel his hugs, even when we strike out. And, buoyed by that assurance, we must learn to do a little hugging of our own.

———————

Mary opened her eyes, squinting into the shafts of sun that spilled through her windows. Already the town of Magdala was bustling, noisily stretching itself to begin another day's fishing. But today was no ordinary day for Mary Magdalene. Yesterday she had felt the touch of the Healer from Galilee, and now her days would be forever different.

Whenever I think of love, love overt and endless, I think of Mary Magdalene. An influential woman from Magdala, she played a major role in Christ's ministry and in the Resurrection story. Her love for Jesus is seen repeatedly in her response to his message and his needs. The source of Mary's love is not to the extent of her sin, but rather the depth of her gratitude.

We do not know exactly where Mary first heard Jesus speak, but we do know that one of his miracles was *her* miracle, a miracle of healing. Seven demons that had racked her body and ruined her life were forced to withdraw when God's own Son entered the scene. Can you imagine the joy Mary must have felt? To be free! To know sleep and peace and self-control! No wonder her heart bulged with love for her Savior. She became at once a disciple, giving both her time and her means to support Christ. And that dedicated love continued through controversy and Calvary and beyond.

Biblical scholars dispute whether the woman who poured out the alabaster box of perfume in Luke 7:36-50 was Mary Magdalene or some local woman to whom Jesus had offered forgiveness. Yet the act of love performed for Jesus here, as he ate in the house of Simon the Pharisee, was certainly characteristic of the love Mary demonstrated in other situations.

Simon, being the chief citizen of Bethany, had done his duty by extending a dinner invitation to Jesus. But the offer was all affectation and no affection. The service he gave Jesus was perfunctory rather than polite. He did not greet Jesus with a kiss, as was the custom, and he failed to provide the ordinary courtesy of washing the dirty, tired feet of his guest. Why was Simon so aloof, so rude? Perhaps he was willing to fulfill his social obligation as host, but did not want to appear overly cordial to this controversial itinerant from Galilee. Simon's hospitality was tainted by his obvious lack of love.

Into this scene of terse hypocrisy comes our protagonist. What a different perspective she has! Her whole attitude is one of love. Having abandoned reserve, she approaches Jesus with the courage of a forgiven and full heart. When she sees his dusty feet, she is moved to tears, and with these she washes his neglected feet. She humbles herself and unclasps her hair, letting its tresses serve as her towel. Next the precious ointment spills from its long imprisonment in the alabaster jar, bathing the feet of the Lord with sweet-smelling perfume. But this was no act meant to impress, no sacrifice meant to draw attention to itself. It was, instead, a lavish outpouring of love from one who had considered herself unlovable. It was generosity and contrition and gratitude. Some criticized her "wastefulness"; the nard she poured out was worth more than a year's salary. But often love demands extravagance—in effort or time or commitment.

Mary Magdalene was one of the faithful few who stood at the foot of Jesus' cross. By this time, all seemed lost. She had nothing to gain by aligning herself with a convicted rebel. No doubt she was exposed to both insult and violence. She may have been pushed away from the cross repeatedly, until finally the crowd grew tired of the sport and left her to her misery. Only love made her persist in the face of peril and horror and hopelessness.

On Holy Saturday night, Mary lovingly prepared the spices that would complete Christ's burial. Then, even before dawn, she made her way toward the tomb. She did not know how she would roll away the huge stone; she only knew what had to be done. But the stone was gone, and so was the body of Jesus. Confused and angry, exhausted from her labors and lack of sleep, Mary remained at the tomb when the other women had gone. Her love was persistent. When Christ appeared, she thought he was the gardener, and she begged to know where the body had been taken. It was only when Christ called her name that she knew: The Lord had risen! Love had triumphed even over death. "Go and tell my disciples," he commanded her.

The Greeks call Mary the "Apostle of the Resurrection to the Apostles." How quickly she must have run with the good news of resurrection! How amply her ceaseless love and care of the Master had been repaid.

Mary of Magdala—her love was bold and tender-hearted, contrite and lavish, open and generous. In her we see our example of selfless, complete love. She is our inspiration for a love that persists, for true love burns not with bursts of flame and color, but rather with constant fires fueled by the love of God.

On a rainy night in 1916, evangelist Charles Weigle watched the westbound train pull out of Sebring, Florida. He strained to see his daughter's face just one more time, but her mother was quick to pull down the shade of the small window.

As he stood on the platform that night, Weigle had never felt so alone. He had given his entire life to spreading the gospel, and it had cost him his marriage. His wife was leaving him for California and what she called "the bright lights." Despondent and desperate, Charles Weigle tried to take his own life that night by hurling himself into the raging waters of Biscayne Bay. But God sustained him, and years later, looking back on that time of anguish and loneliness, Weigle would write the stirring hymn "No One Ever Cared for Me Like Jesus." The first stanza reveals the source of its inspiration.

> I would love to tell you what I think of Jesus,
> Since I found in Him a friend so strong and true;
> I would tell you how he changed my life completely,
> He did something that no other friend could do.

Charles Weigle was awed that God should choose to love him. But God chooses consistently to love each one of us, regardless. The chorus echoes the wonder of it all.

No one ever cared for me like Jesus.
There's no other friend so kind as he.
No one else could take the sin and darkness from me.
Oh, how much he cares for me!

God's love—it sustained Charles Weigle when human love failed, when devotion and dreams lay in crushed piles at his feet. It sustains us today, in the midst of international—and internal—crises. It is God's love—constant, strong, universal—that gives us the strength to love others. The Holy Spirit nudges us to be a friend "so strong and true," to reach out to those flailed by the fickle, selfish nature of earthly love.

---

I stepped into the office, my head throbbing with that familiar end-of-the-day ache. In the halls, high schoolers jostled and joked, yelled and yahooed their way out of the doors and onto waiting buses. Another day. I decided to check my mailbox before going back to my room and that stack of compositions waiting to be graded.

Grading. The papers were endless, and my well-made lesson plans never seemed quite so well made when I tried to present them to a group of lively sophomores. I had been teaching for four weeks and was beginning to sense the awesomeness of my undertaking. Many times I wanted to throw down my red pen and give up.

There was only one piece of mail in my box. It was a photocopied cartoon of an exhausted teacher. Her eyes were bleary, her hair frazzled. She was sitting at her desk, facing an avalanche of paperwork. The caption underneath read: "No one said it was going to be easy." I thought back to my education professors, to my critic teacher, to the administrator who hired me. No one ever said it would be easy. Smiling, I took a new red pen from the supply cabinet and headed toward my room.

Loving is not easy. For every lovable person in your life,

a swarm of unlovables hovers nearby. But it is possible, through the power of the Holy Spirit, to bear the fruit of love. Sink your roots deep into God's love. Stop worrying about being loved; devote your energies to *loving.*

Philippians 1:9-11 expresses Paul's concern that Christians undertake the difficult task of loving.

And this is my prayer: that your love may abound more and more in knowledge and depth of insight, so that you may be able to discern what is best and may be pure and blameless until the day of Christ, filled with the fruit of righteousness that comes through Jesus Christ—to the glory and praise of God.

Christian love is not blind or wishy-washy or shallow. It is, rather, the incarnation of wisdom and insight. Love is both our shield and our weapon in a world of selfishness, greed, and hypocrisy.

But no one said it was going to be easy. Few worthwhile things are. But loving is imperative. "Love one another" is not just a verse for preschoolers or a phrase that needlepoints nicely. It is a way of life, the way of life chosen by Christ. It must become our way of life, too. "The fruit of the Spirit is love. . . ."

# CHAPTER TWO

*Often I am inclined to think that joy is the motor,*
*the thing that keeps everything else going. Joy*
*begets joy.*
    Richard J. Foster, *Celebration of Discipline*

# J O Y

JOY. AT CHRISTMASTIME IT HANGS IN BOLD GOLD LETTERS from ecclesiastical banners and shopping mall ceilings. Carolers proclaim, "Joy to the World!" Christmas cards wish us, "Joyous Holidays!" And for that brief period, joy becomes a household word.

But then a strange and sad thing happens. Christmas is over. We pack away the tinsel and the crêche—and the joy. We return to our routines and ruts, to our grumbling and mumbling. Predictable? Yes. Inevitable? No. Joy need not be a seasonal item, like candy canes and silver tinsel and angels with polyester wings.

True joy is an integral part of the Spirit-filled life. It is the gladness that radiates from the redeemed; it is the delight that dances in the eyes of those who have met Jesus face to face. Christian joy lasts past Christmas— through the muck of March, the swelter of July, the freezing rains of November. Why? Because our source of joy is not the celebration of Christmas; it is the Christ of Christmas.

Skeptical society tends to look on joyful people with suspicion, judging them either simple-minded or just overly simplistic. This erroneous attitude results from mistaking joy for happiness. Truly, no one can be happy twenty-four hours a day. By its very definition, happiness

26

is a response to what happens to us. Reunions make us happy; tax refunds make us happy; a clean bill of health makes us happy. But joy is not a response to what happens to us; it is a response to the One in control of what happens to us.

We are called to be joyful because of Christ. First Peter 1:8 says, "Though you have not seen him, you love him; and even though you do not see him now, you believe in him and are filled with an inexpressible and glorious joy, for you are receiving the goal of your faith, the salvation of your souls." Salvation—what a reason to rejoice! Joy is the natural outlet of the celebration God has placed in our hearts through the indwelling of his Son.

While in prison, Paul wrote a memorable letter to the church at Philippi, encouraging the members to stand firm and to rejoice. But he knew admonitions were useless without sufficient proof as to *why* these early Christians should be joyful. So, like the excellent orator he was, Paul saved this most important point until the end of his letter. In the final chapter of Philippians, he gives the real reason why joy was not only possible, but also logical. "And my God will meet all your needs according to his glorious riches in Christ Jesus" (4:19). *All* our needs. Physical and emotional, whether shoes for the kids or comfort for the heart—God will meet all our needs. What more could we ask? What could make our joy more complete than knowing this?

Believing it, that's what. We must believe in our hearts the truth of God's loving provision for each of us, for in so doing we open ourselves to true joy. Joy is not a mask we tape onto our faces, but rather a source we tap into by turning our eyes fully upon God in all his forgiving majesty and powerful availability.

My teen-aged daughter keeps me tuned in to the latest trends in fashion. Bright ads for name-dropper clothes cover her bulletin board. Window shopping has become her favorite outdoor sport. She pleads for jeans with strange labels and exorbitant prices.

Most of us are, at least, somewhat clothes conscious. We don't wear dress shirts to the beach or grass-stained sneakers to church. In Isaiah 61, we are shown a special "designer fashion" God has for each of us. The prophet tells us that the "Spirit of the Sovereign Lord" waits to bestow on us "a garment of praise instead of a spirit of despair" (v. 3). God would have us wrap ourselves in joyful praise.

If every morning we will consciously put on this garment, making joy our deliberate choice, everything that happens to us must come through this divine buffer. We can then see with renewed vision the closeness and wonder of God. David praises God's ability to change attitudes and emotions: "You turned my wailing into dancing; you removed my sackcloth and clothed me with joy" (Psalm 30:11).

Garments of praise, clothes of joy. What have *you* been wearing lately?

I grew up in a small Midwestern farming community. People were friendly, and neighbors helped neighbors. My grandmother lived with us, and her Kentucky ways fit right in with the lend-a-hand way we all lived. Often a farmer would walk across the field to borrow a tool or a tractor. Sometimes a child would appear on our porch with a quart jar, asking for a cup of sugar or a few pinches of salt. Or an apron-clad housewife would stop by to borrow "a good-sized onion."

Grandma always filled these requests—and then added a little something extra. If the neighbors needed a stick of butter, Grandma would give them a stick and a half. If they asked for a jar of tomatoes, she gave them two. When the garden was in season, and we sold produce to passers-by, Grandma delighted in giving thirteen ears of corn to every dozen or a few extra cucumbers to every peck. I asked her one day why she always gave people more than they asked for, more than they deserved. "Why, that's what we call 'holiness measure,' child," she said, wiping her hands on her apron and taking me into her lap. "It's our duty to share with our fellow creatures here on earth, but it's our *joy* to give them more than they asked for!"

It was years later that I came across John 15:11 in my King James Bible. Jesus was talking to his disciples, saying, "These things have I spoken unto you, that my joy might remain in you, and that your joy might be full" (KJV). *Full*—that was Grandma's idea of "holiness measure." Nothing scanty or selfish, but overflowing and abundant. That's the measure of joy God has for us. Pressed down and running over, more than we ask for or deserve.

Part of what robs Christians today of spontaneous joy in the Spirit is a preoccupation with duty. We go to church out of duty. We teach a Sunday school class out of duty. We visit the nursing homes out of duty. We pray and fast out of duty. Like the Pharisees, we are *so* good, so good and so pious and so imprisoned by deeds done without delight.

For her first birthday, I gave my daughter Amy Jo a big, bright picture book titled simply *Prayers*. We read it often, and it soon became one of her favorites. She would get the book and sit on the floor with the pages open across her legs. Then, bringing her hands together with a loud clap, she would shout, "Pray!" More handclapping and usually a few giggles followed. "Pray!" What joy she had! What freedom of expression! She had not yet learned liturgies and solemnities; she had not yet shouldered the

serious burden of doing "good" things from a sense of
duty.

God's will for his children is that we know the same joy
in serving and praising that Amy Jo had those mornings
as she clapped her hands in prayer. The Pharisees of his
time exasperated and angered Christ. How much more
must we when we assume a joyless service marked by
piety and self-pity! Psalm 47 begins with the words, "Clap
your hands, all you nations; shout to God with cries of
joy." It is not plaintive complaints or endless wants, but
cries of joy that are to be the substance of our prayers. If
only we will make it so, we'll find our lives, and our
service, filled with that same welcome commodity.

Isaiah 35 is nearly poetic as it paints the picture of a
renewed land and a restored people. It predicts the Jews'
return to their homeland from Babylonian exile. Such
imagery!

> Water will gush forth in the wilderness
>   and streams in the desert.
> The burning sand will become a pool,
>   the thirsty ground bubbling springs.
> In the haunts where jackals once lay,
>   grass and reeds and papyrus will grow.
>                                    Isaiah 35:6*b*-7

The indwelling of the Holy Spirit effects a similar change.
A "desert" personality is changed to a "spring" personality. Bits of joy, scarce as desert dew, are replaced with
rivulets of running water from a sure Source.

When I was a little girl, my parents took me to visit
some of our kinfolk back in the hills of Kentucky. This
assortment of aunts and uncles and cousins lived in the
"holler" between two huge, pine-laden mountains. They
had just built a lovely new house from limestone, quarried
there on their own property. I was surprised to see

modern conveniences, including inside plumbing and running water. In fact, it was *very* running water. From the faucets in both the kitchen and bathroom, water ran constantly: gurgle, gurgle, gurgle. Constantly. I was amazed that no one went to turn off the water. But then my cousin explained it to me.

Their water source was a spring in the side of the mountain behind their house. It bubbled into the pipe, sending a nonstop supply of water into the faucets of their house. Nonstop. They were not dependent on rain for their supply of water or electricity to pump it into their sinks and tub. Circumstances were irrelevant; their supply was sure.

Are you struggling on "thirsty ground"? Perhaps you need to renew your contact with the source of bubbling springs, of endless joy. Isaiah ends his 35th chapter with this promise for the redeemed: "Gladness and joy will overtake them, and sorrow and sighing will flee away" (v. 10*b*). Stop striving and struggling. Reach up in praise and wait for the blessings to flow, for joy to overtake you. You won't have long to wait.

It was a miserable March day. Rain thudded against my kitchen window; the skies were the color of muddy galoshes. Small, dirty mounds of snow dotted the yard. On impulse, I called a good friend who lived several states away.

"How's the weather there?" I asked, adding, "It's really awful here!"

"It's lovely!" she replied. "It's raining."

I told her it was raining here, too, but that things were *so ugly*.

"Ah," she replied, "but the rain will rid us of the snow, and that's the first step toward spring."

Long after that phone conversation ended, I thought about her words. I had resented the cold rain, but had not wanted a "first step." What I had wanted was to glide from sparkling, snowy, Christmas-card-perfect winter into a green, radiant, daffodil-filled spring. What I saw as an ugly, colorless scene, my friend saw as a prelude to spring.

Our attitudes and moods are determined not so much by external circumstances, but rather by internal reactions to those circumstances. The writer of Proverbs tells us that "A cheerful look brings joy to the heart" (15:30). A cheerful outlook can be a source of joy, too, if only we will live our lives in search of rainbows instead of storm clouds.

Jan Suffolk Todd has no trouble lifting heavy trash bags, rearranging the living room furniture, or even hoisting her husband onto her shoulders. Jan is a weight lifter, a power-lifter. Her career has included incredible feats of strength. In 1981 she set the world record power lift for a woman. A year later, and eighty-two pounds thinner, Jan was able to set a new world record with a headlift of 446 pounds. Never before in sports history had anyone set records in two classes, five body weights apart!

Strength. In our age of push buttons and keyboards, it's still a valued asset. Biceps and triceps and quadrilaterals tense and grow strong as men and women work out, increasing their strength and endurance. Health foods, fitness centers, self-discipline—all can help us to be physically well and strong.

Strength is important in our spiritual lives, too. Where do we get the strength to stand firm for Christian values in a world of greed and lust? How can we have the strength to do the right, instead of the easy, thing? Nehemiah 8:10 tells us that "the joy of the Lord is your strength." The joy of the Lord. We are able to live daily lives of consecration and service not by gritting our teeth and squaring our jaws, but by being filled with the joy that is born of praise and love and his indwelling.

As Stephen stood outside waiting for Peter, he watched twilight settle on Jerusalem. Inside, the room buzzed with the sounds of the evening meal. Rough benches scraped against the dirt floor. Friendly laughter shook the shoulders of sinewy workers as they shared stories of their day. Women and children filed in through the open door. It seemed as though the whole city were crowded into that stuffy chamber!

Zikkos sat at the far end of the last table, next to his mother and the other Greek women. She held him close to her as she eyed the communal pot of mutton on the middle of the long table. Zikkos was hungry. Last night there had not been enough food to go around, and his mother and the other Greek widows had had to share their small portions with their children. It had happened before, too. Zikkos felt his mouth begin to water as the smell of boiled meat drifted toward him. He hoped that tonight there would be enough for everyone!

Only a few months after the crucifixion, the apostles returned to Jerusalem to found a community of believers in the Messiah. Led by Peter, they all agreed to share everything; nothing was to be held back. Each person's need was to be met through the generosity of this body of Christ. For some time things went well. God blessed their contributions. Barnabas sold a large field and laid the entire sum at the apostles' feet.

But then came the incident with Ananias and Sapphira. Together they covenanted to deceive the others by holding back for themselves money consecrated to the church. The end result was disastrous. Confronted with their sin by Peter, both had fallen dead, smitten of God. So a great fear of the Lord fell on the church, and their numbers grew daily.

As the community of disciples increased, distribution of food became a problem. The Greek Jews felt slighted in their provision. They looked at the Aramaic-speaking Jews with distrust. Why were their plates fuller, their children plump and rosy? Why were the Greek widows always the last to be served? The matter had, at last, been taken up with the apostles themselves.

Suddenly, the room grew quiet. Zikkos looked up to see Peter standing in the doorway. "Dear friends," Peter began, his voice booming across the low-ceilinged room, "with God's help we have appointed seven men to see to the distribution of food among us. These believers are full of the Spirit and wisdom. They will see that each one of you is treated fairly and that no one goes hungry." Whispers pulsed across the tables. Zikkos' mother and the other Greek widows looked at one another hopefully. Zikkos felt his stomach churn. "And now," Peter continued, "let us pray."

As soon as Peter's blessing was complete, the seven men moved into action, filling bowls, passing slices of bread, allotting clusters of grapes and handfuls of figs. Zikkos watched as one of the stewards came toward their table. Peter had called him Stephen. Under his arm, Stephen carried a big wooden bowl filled with broken pieces of cheese. His eyes were serious and merry at the same time. After bowing to his fellow Greeks, Stephen approached Zikkos. "And now, my fine man, would you like a piece of cheese?" Zikkos nodded, and Stephen placed a hunk on the corner of his plate. Then Stephen began serving the others, wearing a smile that began deep inside and lingered playfully around the corners of his mouth.

Joy. Whether serving tables, performing miracles, expounding scriptures, or defending himself before false witnesses and biased tribunals, Stephen was the embodiment of joy. Whatever he did, he did with vigor and enthusiasm! There was nothing lethargic or noncommital about Stephen, nothing half-hearted or apologetic in his approach to life in Christ.

Most of us remember Stephen as the first Christian martyr. When I was a child, on the wall of my Sunday school classroom hung a picture titled *The Stoning of Stephen.* Dark men with angry faces clutched jagged rocks in their hands, waiting to begin the avalanche of pain and disgrace that would end Stephen's life. In the corner of the picture stood a tall young man, holding the cloaks of the others until they had finished their gruesome business. Later I learned that this man was Saul, destined to become Paul—preacher, writer, and himself a martyr for the cause of Christ.

But what I remember most about that picture is Stephen and the look on his face. He was not afraid or angry or oblivious. He was looking up into the clouds, and his whole countenance shone with a gentle radiance. How impressed I was with his appearance, with that almost happy look! And I wasn't the only one. Even his accusers had to take notice.

Stephen's trial before the Sanhedrin in Acts, chapters 6 and 7, closely mirrors the trial of Christ. False witnesses were called, who swore to trumped up charges of blasphemy. As did his Savior before him, Stephen defended himself with scripture, while at the same time holding firm to his proclamation of the Messiahship of Christ. How did Stephen look during this trying ordeal, while scribes scribbled false evidence and students of the law stroked their beards in disgust? Acts 6:15 tells us: "All who were sitting in the Sanhedrin looked intently at Stephen, and they saw that his face was like the face of an angel."

What, exactly, does the face of an angel look like? Joyful! What other expression could be found on the very beings who stand in the presence of God? What consternation Stephen's joy must have brought to those pious, pitiful religious leaders of his day! Their power over him was temporal, while his source of joy was eternal.

And then it was over. The stones had been hurled. Raw gashes oozed fresh blood. Stephen left this world the same way he lived in it—with compassion and assurance and *joy*. Stephen's last sight was of Jesus standing at the right hand of God, waiting to receive his spirit. Stephen's last thoughts were of his executioners: "Lord, do not hold this sin against them" (Acts 7:60). Even in the grip of a painful, unjust death, Stephen knew the joy of the Lord, a joy so complete that it could wish no harm to anyone.

Stephen—he has more to teach us than how to die courageously. His life is an example of how to live joyously!

---

Ina folded her silk dresses into the trunk. Their bright ribbons and delicate laces felt strangely foreign to her fingertips. She read, again, the telegram that had arrived yesterday. "Father is ill. Please come home." She blinked back tears as her ears filled with the remembered applause of appreciative audiences.

Ina Ogdon was a woman of both talent and personality. Her voice, her stage presence, her illustrious start—all pointed to a great future in the theater. Then came that life-changing, dream-shattering telegram.

So home she went to look after her invalid father. Ina's stage was now her kitchen floor and the confines of the sickroom. Her audience was reduced to family (a group, in any era, noted for its critics!). And her song? Did it shrivel into the bitterness of her soul? Hardly! She determined to let her light shine, even without the glare of stage lights. She not only learned the lesson of unconditional joy, but also taught it, by contagion, to those around her.

Then, in 1913, Ina Ogden put her philosophy into poetic form by writing the gospel song "Brighten the Corner Where You Are." Its chorus admonished:

> Brighten the corner where you are.
> Brighten the corner where you are.
> Someone far from harbor
> You may guide across the bar.
> Brighten the corner where you are!

First sung at a great meeting in Syracuse, New York, the song met with instant and wide acceptance. The girl who left the public pleasure of performing for the private task of service soon found her tune, and her name, on the lips of people everywhere.

Joy. It's hard to counterfeit, impossible to conceal. Why not brighten whatever "corners" you frequent today?

---

Election week was always an exciting time on campus. Dormitory lawns sprouted hand-painted signs with catchy campaign slogans. My friend Joy was running for class president that year, and together we had been up all night making signs. We had readied sets of them to be placed along the walks between various campus buildings. They were written in the "Burma Shave" tradition—several signs placed within a short distance of one another, each message building toward the final sign. Arranged in sets of four, they read:

> If you want joy,
> real joy,
> wonderful joy—
> VOTE FOR HER!

I remember those signs sometimes—when I'm swamped with work, accosted with criticism, tired of trying, weighted with the woes of a sinsick world. *Joy*. It's there for us; we need only accept the fullness of Christ, keep close to the Word, and let the Holy Spirit work through us.

Do you want joy, real joy, wonderful joy? Reach up for it. Expect it. Vote for it to fill your life!

Several years ago, my husband and I bought an answering machine. Now, whenever we're away from the phone, its mechanical voice greets our callers and records their messages. Many people simply hang up. Others preface their message with "I hate these machines!" And one of my friends has been known to leave comic renditions of her answering machine talking to mine.

Messages. For centuries they have brought news of battles and treaties, of true love and infidelity, of trivial and triumphant affairs. But no other message has brought with it the repercussions of that heavenly proclamation delivered to common shepherds huddled on Judean hills: "I bring you the most joyful news ever announced, and it is for everyone! The Savior—yes, the Messiah, the Lord—has been born tonight in Bethlehem!" (Luke 20:10*b*-11 TLB).

The Messiah! Nothing would ever be the same again. Through Christ's blood God would reconcile the weary world. Sadness and sighing would flee away. No more must mortals spend their days in strife and empty striving. God's own Son had come to give them abundant life, a heavenly inheritance, a divine mission.

"The most joyous news ever announced" is still being proclaimed. It resounds from pulpits and street corners. It whispers in the love of Christians for their fellow creatures. It laughs in the lives of those filled with his presence. "The fruit of the Spirit is . . . joy."

---

# CHAPTER THREE

*Thou hast made us for Thyself, and the heart of man
is restless until it finds its rest in Thee.*
St. Augustine, *Confessions*

# PEACE

---

$P$EACE. THAT WAS THE ONE WORD THAT FILLED FERDINAND
Magellan's mind as he gazed at the calm water lapping on
either side of his battered vessel. The date was 1520, and
for over a year Magellan had battled vicious storms,
mutinous crews, and false hopes in his search for a
passage through South America and into the southern
seas beyond. Now, finally, such a passage had been
found. It had taken thirty-eight days to manuever his
ships through the over 360 miles of icy water, narrow
straits, and winding borders. When at last Magellan and
his exhausted crew sailed into the welcome vastness of
the open ocean, they were overcome with a sense of relief
and peace. And so Ferdinand Magellan called the great
body of water the Pacific, or peaceful, Ocean. His men
lifted their faces to the sun and offered thanks to God for
safety and success and the prospect of peaceful days.

In any age, peace is a sought-after possession. Anti-war
groups protest for it; churches proclaim special days to pray
for it; philosophers and economists and presidential
advisors expound upon its possibilities. In our day of nuclear
testing and outer space potential, peace has become a
common headline in the evening papers. But what, really, is
peace? Simply the absence of war? Or does it entail more
than a scarcity of battles and bombings and blood?

Peace is harmony. It is the orchestration of daily stress and tension, of conflicting goals and aspirations. Peace is freedom from the dissension and dissonance of self-serving attitudes. In our world of nationalistic and ambitious people, peace can be an elusive and misunderstood goal.

Peace was an integral part of Christ's message during his time here on earth. Into the Roman world of clashing swords and tramping feet, Christ came. Even his advent held overtones of conflict, because Bethlehem had originally been built by the Canaanites to honor Lahum, their god of war. And here the Prince of Peace was born! In his Sermon on the Mount, Christ extolled the virtues of peacemakers, calling them "blessed" and "sons of God." After his resurrection, when he appeared to his frightened and confused disciples, Christ's first word was "Peace!" They had waited for him to raise an army, to strike a blow, to establish God's kingdom on earth. It took Christ's brutal death, his miraculous resurrection, his appearance, and his ascension before those disciples came to realize that God's kingdom was within. So also was the peace they could now claim through Christ.

Isaiah 53 is sometimes called "the fifth gospel" because it portrays so vividly the person and mission of Christ.

> Surely he took up our infirmities
>    and carried our sorrows,
> yet we considered him stricken by God,
>    smitten by him, and afflicted.
> But he was pierced for our transgressions,
>    he was crushed for our iniquities;
> the punishment that brought us peace
>       was upon him,
>    and by his wounds we are healed.
>                                 Isaiah 53:4-5

His punishment bought our peace. In a world of want and war and striving, we are called to both know and promote peace through Christ's atonement.

Someone once told me, "You can counterfeit all the fruits of the Spirit except one: Peace." It's true. We can, like the Pharisees, make an outward show of righteousness. But peace is not to be feigned. It is the gift of God to the believer; it is the indwelling calm that does not depend on circumstance. Colossians 1:19-20 echoes the truth of Isaiah's prophecy: "For God was pleased to have all his fullness dwell in [Christ], and through him to reconcile to himself all things, whether things on earth or things in heaven, by making peace through his blood, shed on the cross." Through the sacrifice of God's own son, we have been reconciled, granted not only pardon but also peace.

When I was a child, I was required to read two chapters in the Bible every day. I can remember as a six-year-old holding Mother's big King James Bible on my lap and making my way through those chapters word by word. For obvious reasons, I came to love the Psalms. I often read certain New Testament chapters over and over, until I had inadvertently memorized an entire passage. Such a chapter was John 14. I could visualize Jesus talking with his disciples, the tweve of them leaning over to catch his every word. Soon they were to face the greatest crisis of their lives. Yet his promise to them was: "Peace I leave with you; my peace I give you. I do not give to you as the world gives. Do not let your hearts be troubled and do not be afraid" (v. 27). Christ's gift was not of this world; it was generous and permanent and perfect. Christ's bequest to his followers is peace. Then. Now. Always.

I enjoy nature; everything from "wooly worms" to apple blossoms intrigues me. So much of nature is filled with awe and mystery! I am reminded of that every spring when our kindergarten Sunday schoolers plant their beans.

On the last Sunday of March, the children are given small cups filled with dirt. Then, with chubby fingers, they push the beans deep into the rich potting soil. After the cups have been labeled with the children's names, we place them on the window sill. And there they sit, silent cups of dirt. But Sundays pass, and underneath the soil the beans are changing, emerging, growing. Then one sunny morning, as all the children crowd around to once again inspect the dirt, someone notices a tiny green shoot sticking shyly up from the black soil. The room erupts with squeals and cheers and clapping, while my own heart grows full with the wonder of it all, a wonder I can never really grasp.

I sometimes have trouble understanding the things of God, too. Philippians 4:7 tells us that the peace of God "transcends all understanding." It is beyond human capacity to comprehend this gift of calm and quiet that saturates the soul. We can never fully understand it, but we can accept and experience it, simply by opening our hearts to the Holy Spirit in all its fullness.

According to one authority, this world of ours has been beset by war somewhere on an average of one every three years for over 3,000 years. What a staggering statistic— and probably woefully accurate. Many of these conflicts were resolved, after bloody and needless waste, through the efforts of mediators. Peace is often the result of someone's stepping between warring factions and negotiating the terms of settlement. Frequently, compromise is involved; often concessions are made. But never again is the world of either victor or victim the same.

Christ is the mediator between fallen man and God. It is through him that we are justified. A Sunday school teacher once explained *justified* this way. "Through the sacrificial blood of Jesus Christ, we are brought into a right relationship with God. Then Christ's love goes even further, by justifying us, by making it *just-as-if* we'd never sinned." Christ restores us to a state of perfection in the eyes of God. Unlike earthly mediators, Christ is able to recreate a state of perfect peace, as if conflict never existed. "Therefore, since we have been justified through faith, we have peace with God through our Lord Jesus Christ, through whom we have gained access by faith into this grace in which we now stand" (Romans 5:1-2*a*). Peace with God—a state always accompanied by peace with ourselves, too.

We live in an age of specialists. Lawyers specialize; engineers specialize; educators specialize. The family doctor has been replaced by a pediatrician, a gynecologist, a neurologist, a podiatrist—the list is endless. And each one knows precisely what to prescribe for an infinite number of illnesses and injuries associated with his or her field. Whether they prescribe capsules, ointments, or regimens, we take seriously the advice of these experts.

The Bible has its own prescription for a healthy body: "A heart at peace gives life to the body" (Proverbs 14:30). Nothing is more destructive to your physical well-being than inner turmoil and constant conflict. God (a noted expert!) has written your prescription:

Rx: One heart at peace

The bill has been paid for you. All you need do is claim what's already yours.

It was written at the bottom of the tube in tiny letters, but neither my daughter nor I paid any real attention to it. Not until the earring incident.

Amy Jo is forever breaking the posts off her earrings. So I invested in a small tube of glue that boasted of binding together cracked toys and displaced jewels and broken pots. One morning, in a hurry to mend her earring and still catch the school bus, Amy Jo glued the small metal post to the back of the earring, immediately inserted it through her lobe, and left for school. By 3:00 P.M., the earring was firmly connected to her ear. It was then, while she cried and I attempted to gently wrench the ornament away from her ear, that we read the small print on the tube: INSTANTLY BONDS SKIN. We spent the next several hours dousing the lobe with fingernail polish remover, alcohol, vinegar, turpentine, and even a slimy substance used to loosen bolts and nuts. Finally, we were able to pry the earring loose. By then we were both firm believers in the potency, and near permanency, of that high-powered glue.

Bonding. It's salvaged many broken teapots, created many hand-cut-and-colored cards. Peace is a bonding agent, too. Its purpose? To keep the unity of the Spirit, to bind us closer to one another and to God. Ephesians 4:3 reads: "Make every effort to keep the unity of the Spirit through the bond of peace." The shards of relationships, the cutting edges of differing opinions—all that would rift the body of Christ can be bonded with the unity born of peace.

I love sending and receiving Christmas cards. Every year, as I pack away my Christmas decorations and keepsakes, I choose one card to sit on my bookshelf during the coming year. It helps remind me of the wonder of Christ's birth and of the selflessness of the Christmas spirit. Some years I select a card for its scene; other times it's the message that speaks to me through those long months between Advent seasons. Last year's card had a simple sketch of a lion and a lamb lying side by side. I'd seen that picture hundreds of times before, but it was the verse inside that struck me so powerfully: "Let there be peace on earth and let it begin with me."

I remember singing that line in a school concert long ago. *Let it begin with me.* If each one of us would pray that prayer, what a difference it could make in our world! We just might change those statistics on war, one conflict at a time.

Sometimes I think the changing of seasons is marked not so much by nature as by the kinds of sports shoes my children clamor for. Every activity seems to need a special shoe. There is no doubt a huge conspiracy to keep some company from coming out with *the* shoe that could see a child through every sport. The floors of my children's closets are covered with piles of tennis shoes, baseball cleats, running shoes, basketball high tops, wrestling shoes. What the world really needs is a rebate system for out-grown, lost-the-mate-to, worn-out, lost-interest-in-the-sport, change-of-season shoes!

Admittedly, shoes are important for athletes and would-be athletes. They're important for nurses and models and door-to-door salesmen. They're important for soldiers, too. In Ephesians, Paul talks about the apparel necessary for a soldier of Christ—the belt of truth, the breastplate of righteousness, the helmet of salvation, the shield of faith, the sword of the Spirit. And on the feet? "Stand firm then . . . with your feet fitted with the readiness that comes from the gospel of peace" (6:14-15). We Christians, as we fight God's battles, are not to wear combat boots, but rather, as the Living Bible puts it, "shoes that are able to speed you on as you preach the Good News of peace with God" (Ephesians 6:15).

Footwear really does make a difference. I feel absolutely glamorous when I wear my red high heels. Nothing is more irritating or fatiguing than working all day in a pair of ill-fitting shoes. Cleats give essential grip on a muddy soccer field. Shoes—they affect how we look, how we feel, and how we perform. No wonder God has shod our feet with peace!

---

Abigail woke before dawn, the bleating of the sheep loud and insistent. She rose in the close darkness of her bedchamber and dressed quickly, starting for the servants' quarters as soon as she had strapped on her last sandal. Today the sheepshearing began, and Abigail had to see that the men feasted in a style becoming a man of her husband's wealth. At the last count, Nabal had bragged of owning three thousand sheep, besides the other livestock. Abigail sighed. If only her husband were as wise as he were rich! His surly attitude often offended people; his foolishness and selfishness were common knowledge. But surely today he would be in a good mood! It had been a prosperous season. The shepherds had lost few of the sheep to the constant marauding nomads. The herdsmen had spoken highly of one David, the warrior, and his men who were in hiding in the hills. David's band had helped protect Nabal's herds and servants; the men had literally been a wall of protection around his herdsmen.

Abigail thought fleetingly of David, the one who had been anointed already by the prophet Samuel to be the next king of Israel. Perhaps David and his men would join the day's festivities. It would be only fair, since they had aided in caring for the flocks. Abigail would be sure she had enough to show their gratitude and hospitality. "Come!" she called, clapping her hands at the servant. "We have much to do—bread to bake and meat to dress and water to draw. Quickly!"

Abigail was a woman of rare stamina and foresight. First Samuel 25:3 describes her as an "intelligent and beautiful woman." But like Beauty and the Beast, she was mismatched to a spouse who was "surly and mean in his dealings." Even his name, Nabal, meant "fool"! And his actions on this feast day of sheepshearing were in keeping with his stupidity and selfishness.

David was running for his life from the irrational and evil Saul. With his following of six hundred men, David had taken refuge in the scrubby grassland of Moan, living in strongholds of the hills, helping to protect local shepherds from cut-throat nomads. But his supplies were running low. So when he heard that Nabal, the richest man in all the land, was shearing his sheep, David sent ten of his men to ask for their rightful part of the feast. They should have been welcome. It was a reasonable request. David and his men had not only helped Nabal's herdsmen, but also had never once plundered their camp or demanded payment. Now David asked for only what food his ten men could carry. It was a most reasonable request, but Nabal was not a reasonable man. In a state of drunken bravado, he not only refused to give David food, but also insulted him and his band of loyal followers, saying: "Who is this David? Who is this son of Jesse? Many servants are breaking away from their masters these days. Why should I take my bread and water, and the meat I have slaughtered for my shearers, and give it to men coming from who knows where?" (I Samuel 25:10-11).

David's temper was as quick as his arm was strong. When his comrades returned empty-handed with the message of Nabal's rude reply, David at once assembled four hundred of his men, vowing that not one of Nabal's household would be alive by dawn. Swords drawn, they started down the path toward the sounds of merrymaking. Bloodshed, violence, murder—all seemed inevitable. But then came Abigail.

Abigail was a woman of action as well as of wisdom.

Having heard from one of the servants her husband's rash comments, Abigail began at once to prepare gifts of food for David. She knew that a man of his caliber and capabilities would take quick revenge. She spoke not a word of her plan to Nabal, who sat drinking and boasting among the shearers. Soon Abigail was riding up the mountain toward David's camp, followed by donkeys laden with two hundred loaves of bread, five dressed sheep, five bushels of roasted grain, two skins of wine, and one hundred cakes each of raisins and figs.

Then, as she and her caravan rounded a sharp bend in the trail, she found herself face to face with David and his armed band. At once she dismounted and, bowing before him, began to intercede for her foolish husband. She begged David to keep his own hands from vengeful blood, to forgive the smallness of one far his inferior. She called David "master" and ended her eloquent plea with these words: "When the LORD has done for my master every good thing he promised concerning him and has appointed him leader over Israel, my master will not have on his conscience the staggering burden of needless bloodshed or of having avenged himself" (I Samuel 25:30-31a). And as the sounds of Abigail's wise advice echoed off mountain walls, David felt his anger melt.

The story of Abigail and David could have ended with bloodshed and regrets and senseless loss. Instead, God himself struck down the foolish Nabal. David's wrath was appeased, his conscience was clear, and his troops were well fed.

Peace. It's not a passive act. Sometimes it takes more courage to stand for peace than it does to fall into conflict.

---

In November, 1873, the French luxury liner SS *Ville du Havre* sailed out of New York Harbor, while confetti streamed over the side and smiling passengers waved to well-wishers on shore. Among those passengers were Mrs. H. G. Spafford and her four children. Together they had traveled from Chicago to sail on the *Ville du Havre* for a long-awaited trip to the British Isles and then on to continental Europe. So the voyage at last began, with calm waters and crisp, bright air. But after only a few days at sea, tragedy struck. First came the shuddering jolt that sent passengers tumbling from their berths onto the floor. Next came the ripping of timbers and the awful reality of cold water.

The date was November 22; the time was 2:00 A.M. The *Ville du Havre* had been rammed by the British iron sailing boat *Lochearn*.

Mrs. Spafford groped in the darkness for her children, their cries mingling with sounds of rushing water and crashing metal. "Hold on!" she screamed, realizing in horror that there was nothing left to hold onto.

Within two hours it was over. The luxurious French liner had settled to the bottom of the Atlantic. More than 220 lives were lost, including the four Spafford children. It was nine days later, from Wales, that Mrs. Spafford cabled her husand: "Saved Alone."

Mr. Spafford immediately booked passage and began his own grief-filled voyage across the Atlantic to join his wife. He couldn't eat or sleep. He could only stare at the horizon and weep. One evening the captain invited Mr. Spafford into his cabin. "I believe," the captain began hesitantly, "we are now passing over the place where the *Ville du Havre* went down."

That night Mr. Spafford walked the decks. He looked down into the waters that had sucked his children to a dark grave of seaweed and slime. Overcome by grief, he stared for hours into that abyss. But then a remarkable feeling began edging out the despair, and there in the mid-Atlantic, with the loss of his children wringing his heart almost to breaking, H. G. Spafford began to feel a deep peace. It enfolded him and comforted him and ministered to him, urging him to trust the Lord now that it would cost him something to do so.

Mr. Spafford went to his cabin and immediately penned the words that had come to him on deck. Later those stanzas would become one of the church's best-loved hymns of assurance, "It Is Well with My Soul."

> When peace like a river attendeth my way,
> When sorrows like sea billows roll,
> Whatever my lot, Thou has taught me to say,
> "It is well, it is well with my soul."

Grief, sorrow, and bitterness had bowed to the awesome power of God-given peace.

Bearing the fruit of peace means living together peacefully; it means getting along with those people who are obstinate and willful and annoying. Our inner peace through reconciliation with God must be expressed in an outer attitude of peace toward our fellow human beings. Even when that's difficult to do—especially when that's difficult to do.

---

I was teaching seventh-grade language arts, and Larry was in fifth-hour class. He was an action verb personified—rambunctious, energetic, active, maddening. He did not walk; he darted. His pencil would "accidentally" break at least twice an hour, and his trips to the pencil sharpener always featured at least two kicked desks and one trampled book. His work was either camouflaged by erasures or ghost-written with dying ink pens. We were at war, Larry and I. I was determined to domesticate him, to educate him. He was just as determined to have a good time, to get out of assignments. To drive me crazy.

Then, one dreary March afternoon, I looked out at the

class and made a shocking discovery about myself. Everyone was reading the assigned story in his or her literature book. Everyone except Larry, who was busy making a paper airplane. In that moment, I realized that I did not even like this kid. I wanted to humiliate him, to punish him, to subordinate him. And those feelings scared me. So I began to try and find good things about Larry. It wasn't easy, but I knew it was not God's will that Larry and I remain enemies. "Make every effort to live in peace with all men" (Hebrews 12:14). Every . . . all . . .

I began asking Larry for help with classroom chores—passing out papers, watering plants, emptying the pencil sharpener. And slowly, very slowly, my attitude toward him began to change. I learned that Larry had two paper routes and was a champion dirt bike racer. I learned that his parents were separated and that he and his mother lived with his grandmother. I learned to look at Larry as a person, not as an opponent. In his own way, he began to respond to me, too.

I'm not going to tell you that these mutual efforts were a constant or astounding success. Larry did not become a model student; I'm not sure I was the model teacher, either. But we were two people trying to get along, struggling with differences and defenses, making "every effort to live in peace." And that was success enough.

Peace. It's not the absence of pain and conflict in our world; it's the presence of Christ in our lives. "The fruit of the Spirit is . . . peace."

---

# CHAPTER FOUR

*Have courage for the great sorrows of life and
patience for the small ones.*

Victor Hugo

# PATIENCE

---

*P*ATIENCE. THAT WAS THE VIRTUE GRANDMA ADMONISHED ME
to practice as I waited for the strawberries to ripen. It
seemed the closer I watched the plants, the greener the
tiny berries became! "Be patient," she said. "Them
berries are on a schedule all their own, and you trampin'
about in the patch won't hurry them up one bit." But
patience was a hard lesson for me to learn. I wanted my
marigold seeds to sprout and bloom within the week. I
wanted Candy, my white-faced cow, to calf as soon as the
neighbors had loaded up their bull and pulled out of our
drive. But over the years, farming became a good teacher
of patience. I learned that each season had its own charm
as well as its own chores. I learned to savor anticipation
almost as much as realization. I tried hard to heed the
advice of poet Ralph Waldo Emerson: "Adopt the pace of
nature: her secret is patience."

As I grew older, I became impatient to get my driver's
license, to begin dating, to graduate from high school, to
enroll in college. During those adolescent years,
Grandma would often open her Bible and read James
5:7-8 to me: "Be patient. . . . See how the farmer waits for
the land to yield its valuable crop and how patient he is for
the fall and spring rains. You too, be patient and stand
firm." I would take a deep breath and promise to try.

Today, with a husband and two children of my own, I'm still trying. Grocery lines, traffic lights, spilled grape juice, drive-through fast-food pick-ups, dog messes on the back step—all try my patience. We are by nature impatient beasts; yet, God has called us to bear the fruit of patience.

Patience is endurance. It is greeting daily catastrophes with calm; it is meeting injustice without complaint. Patience is that quiet perseverance that separates the sprinters from the marathon runners in the Christian race. To a great extent, patience is the ability to put off justice. You don't blare your horn at the car cutting over in front of you; you don't beat to death the cat that just clawed your new drapes; you don't hang up on your elderly neighbor who is telling you (again!) about his crab grass problem; you don't scream at the kids for breaking the garage window. Patience is the ability to show mercy. It is being not only right, but also *righteous*.

I had an education professor who gave this advice to all would-be teachers: "Never pray for patience!" It seemed a strange warning, until I looked up the scripture that she had cited with her admonition: "tribulation worketh patience" (Romans 5:3 KJV). Tribulation! Certainly that was the last thing we frightened student teachers would pray for. But like metal refined by fire, patience shows its truest character during times of affliction and hardship. It is only through the presence of the Holy Spirit in our lives that we can emerge from trials more tolerant, more courageous, and more patient.

Patience is an integral part of hope. When my local church launched into a much-needed building program, the first structure built was the "family facility," consisting of a gymnasium, a kitchen, and an educational wing. For several years we worshiped in that "sanctinasium" as we came to call our gym-turned-sanctuary. But every Sunday during that time, our church bulletin featured an artist's sketch of the new sanctuary. Every week we were reminded of what we were giving and working and hoping for.

Romans 8:24*b*-25 says, "But hope that is seen is no hope at all. Who hopes for what he already has? But if we hope for what we do not yet have, we wait for it patiently." It is patience that lets us hope for an early spring, a letter from a loved one, a better day tomorrow than we had today, or a soon-to-be-finished sanctuary. The elusive character of hope makes patience essential. If we do not wait with patience, we wait in frustration and striving, our days divided into complaining, anxious moments.

Patience is belief embodied. It is knowing that he who remembers to let the clover bloom will not forget you. It is walking confidently through pain and pandemonium, knowing you are not alone, knowing the end is there, even if out of sight. Patience is wisdom. It is the application of the knowledge of God's abiding and guiding presence. "A man's wisdom gives him patience" (Proverbs 19:11).

My typewriter has a correction tape that "lifts off" my errors, leaving an assorted line of recalled words and letters on the disposable transparent tape. One day my son, Brett, fished one of these out of the trash can near my desk. Slowly, he rolled out the whole thing, until the floor was covered with the see-through line dotted with dark letters. "What are you doing?" I asked.

Looking up, he answered firmly, "Looking at my mommy's mistakes."

I looked closely at this much-loved child. He had been making a lot of mistakes lately—forgetting to water the dog, not taking out the trash, failing his spelling test, breaking my favorite vase. And now he sat at my feet, taking comfort in my mistakes.

Second Timothy 4:2 tells us that we should "correct, rebuke and encourage—with great patience." Sometimes we as parents, and Christians, become obsessed with correcting faults in others, with rebuking actions we consider less than Christlike. But we forget the spirit in which we must do these things: great patience.

I sat down on the floor with Brett and took him into my lap. Together, we both looked at the messy tape. The closeness and the laughter helped correct my unseen mistakes, too.

Clara Barton was a woman of extraordinary stamina and vision. During the Civil War she distributed food and supplies to Union troops. Moved by the misery and horror of the battlefield, Clara volunteered to nurse wounded soldiers at the front of the conflict. Grateful soldiers dubbed her "Angel of the Battlefields." It was through her later persistent and impassioned efforts that the American Red Cross was formed.

Clara Barton was noted not only for her nursing skills and her compassion, but also for her patience in dealing with others. The story is told of a friend who was recalling an injustice rendered to Clara by one of her coworkers. "Don't you remember?" the friend urged.

"No," Clara replied. "I don't."

"But you must!" her friend persisted, recalling in detail the painful situation.

"No," she insisted. "I really don't recollect the incident. But I do distinctly remember forgetting it."

Perhaps Proverbs 15:18 should be our credo in dealing with hurtful situations and thoughtless people: "a patient man calms a quarrel." Then, like Clara Barton, we can be magnanimous instead of petty, charitable instead of challenging.

It was a frigid morning. Ice covered the ground, and a chilling mist beat against exposed skin. Overnight, the campus had been hit by another freezing, wet snow-storm. I hurried toward the science building, silently berating my alarm clock for failing me again. I had to get to class on time! The professor was a fanatic about punctuality. He was also an expert at humiliation if you happened to come in late. I turned up my coat collar and tried to run on the slick pavement.

Suddenly I heard it. The sound was almost lost in the chiming of the campus clock and the howling of the wind. What could be making that strange sound? I unbundled my ears and listened. Someone was crying! I followed the eerie, wind-borne sounds to the back of the administration building.

He looked so small and alone, fighting sobs and wiping tears, wandering back and forth in a path his feet had scuffed in the fresh snow. When he saw me, he stood statue-like, except for left-over sobs.

"Hi," I said. "What's the problem?"

He lifted his chapped face and eyed me intently. No answer.

"Did you lose your gloves?" I asked. He buried his mittenless hands in his coat pockets.

The clock began its ominous 8:30 chiming. My heart sank, but I tried to sound cheerful. "You like snow?"

He stared at me for what seemed a lifetime and then said, "Can't get across the street. I'm terrible late by now." He pointed to his school, accessible only by crossing a busy highway.

I knew just how it felt to be late. "Now what a coincidence," I smiled. "It just happens that I'm crossing this street, too. Think we could walk together?"

I took his small shivering hand in mine and, talking cheerfully, led him safely across. Once in the school yard, he slipped his hand away, rubbed his sleeve across his eyes and runny nose, looked wide-eyed into my face, and bounded away. I watched as he neared the schoolhouse, then turned to face the bitter walk back.

But suddenly I heard his voice, shrill as the wind itself, yelling, "Hey, lady! Hey, lady!" I turned around and looked through the swirling snow at the smiling youngster. He waved both hands wildly over his head and yelled, "Thanks! Thanks a lot!" I waved back as I watched him disappear into the warmth and security of the school building.

Back on campus, I reluctantly neared my classroom door. I could hear the professor lecturing in his authoritative way. I hesitated. Mustering my courage, I eased the door open and attempted to slip into my seat unnoticed. I was not successful.

"Well," the professor boomed. "I see we have someone here this morning who has neither the self-discipline nor the common courtesy to be on time." He grunted and began fumbling with his seating chart. I could feel my cheeks redden. "Do you suppose, Mary Lou, that it was easier for each of us to make it to class than it was for you? You must realize the importance of time. Time properly used . . ."

But the sounds of reprimand blurred to mere background noise as a small voice echoed in my mind. "Thanks, lady. Thanks a lot."

Patience. It keeps us from the burden of prejudging, from the myth of infallibility. It improves both our tolerance and our temperament. It lets us live in the warmth of the Son and not in the Siberia of a selfish soul.

Role models are important in establishing behavior patterns. Hero worship is a common malady of adolescence. Many adults find someone they admire and whose actions they attempt to emulate. It is the courage of the commander that inspires the troops to charge into battle. It is the desire to someday be a major league player that prompts hours of batting practice. I quit swimming lessons the day the instructor ordered us into the deep water while she stood dry and smiling on the side of the pool. I needed someone to *show* me how to brave those twelve-foot depths.

God, himself, is our model of patience. In the person of Christ, he waded into the worries of early life. He met and mastered frustration and injustice. Because of Christ's sacrificial and redemptive death, God now pulls us to himself with cords of patience. He is the epitome of endless wooing and constant caring. Second Peter 3:9*b* says, "[God] is patient with you, not wanting anyone to perish, but everyone to come to repentance." *Everyone.* Like his, our patience must be all-inclusive, encompassing the unlovely and the undeserving.

I enjoy plants. Both friends and family often comment on my "green thumb." My Boston ferns flourish, their fronds tumbling over the sides of clay pots like verdant waterfalls. Weeping figs, philodendron, ivy—for me they all grow with a healthy profusion.

That's why I was upset last year when my Christmas cactus didn't bloom. I had received it as a gift the year before, and then it had been covered with bright red blossoms. Now its leaves were water-spotted and pale. Not even one bud hinted of bloom. Disgusted, I put the cactus behind my parlor palm, where I could water it without really having to look at it.

Several months later, as I was doing my routine watering, a splash of color caught my eye. I reached behind the palm and picked up my Christmas cactus. I could hardly believe my eyes! Plush crimson flowers weighted the leaves. Dozens of tiny buds promised even more blossoms.

I placed it in the center of my kitchen table, where for weeks my family and I enjoyed its beauty. Every time I glanced its way, my heart was stirred with the possibilities of patience, for people as well as for plants.

---

One of my favorite Bible stories is the account of the Great Flood. I can see Noah and his three sons felling the huge cypress trees, hacking off the bark and hewing the trunks into water-worthy planks, while their wicked peers jeered and shouted insults. For years they worked on that boat, in a spot so far inland that a scarcity of water seemed a more impending threat than a profusion of rain. As he hammered and planed and sawed, Noah preached. His topic was always the same: repentance. But his neighbors were more interested in sensual pleasures, in greed and gluttony, in idolatry and innocent bloodshed.

Then the rains began. Drops the size of grapes plopped onto the dust around the ark. Their patter turned to pounding, and inside the ark Noah and his family knew it was true. God was destroying the world. Only they and the animals on board would survive.

For the next year, Noah and the others on the ark lived in a world of bobbing isolation. At first they heard the cries of now-penitent people, the terrified screams of jackals and wolves. But soon these sounds were silenced by the slosh of waves, by the reality of water rising higher than the mountains.

What patience Noah had! During those long years of labor, during those long months of confinement, he did not rant or rail. He waited. He did not pace in panic. He waited. And one morning, as sunlight streamed through the solitary window and patterned the worn deck, Noah knew it was time. He released a dove. She came back by nightfall, unable to find a resting place. For almost a month he sent forth this bird. Although he longed for respite from his watery world—longed to see the rough beauty of tree bark and to feel the earth beneath his feet—Noah knew that this was no time to be impulsive. It was no time to lead the remnants of creation into an unsure situation. Finally, the dove did not return. Then Noah was certain that the ground was indeed dry, that the fury of God's judgment had passed.

The huge door of the ark creaked open. Foxes and camels blinked into the brightness. Birds fluttered their folded wings and fumbled into flight. Lions tossed their manes as memories stirred of star-filled nights spent stalking prey.

What did Noah do? Rush headlong out into this new world? Boast at having beaten the odds? Organize committees to establish a new community? Hardly! "Then Noah built an altar to the LORD and, taking some of all the clean animals and clean birds, he sacrificed burnt offerings on it" (Genesis 8:20). Even in this time of great jubilation, of enormous challenge, Noah's priorities and patience were intact. He paused to offer thanks. And God, pleased with Noah, promised never again to destroy all living creatures.

> "As long as the earth endures,
> seedtime and harvest,
> cold and heat,
> summer and winter,
> day and night
> will never cease."
>
> Genesis 8:22

What did Noah do then? He planted a vineyard, and, sure of God's promise, settled down to watch it grow. To *patiently* watch it grow.

---

It was the middle of the nineteenth century, and Septimus Winner was fast becoming a successful writer of secular songs. Sometimes bawdy, always lively, his music set toes to tapping and coins to jingling as more and more of his pieces were sold.

But then came the Civil War. In its awful backwash, Winner wrote his most popular song. It was far removed from the jocular ditties that characterized his earlier work. It echoed the hopes that the nation, North and South, clung to in this time of transition and sorrow. Winner titled the piece "Whispering Hope" and published it under the pen name Alice Hawthorne.

> Soft as the voice of an angel,
> Breathing a lesson unheard,
> Hope with a gentle persuasion,
> Whispers her comforting word.
> Wait till the darkness is over,
> Wait till the tempest is gone,
> Hope for the sunshine tomorrow,
> After the shower is gone.
>
> *Refrain:*
> Whispering hope,
> Oh how welcome Thy Voice.
> Making my heart,
> in its sorrow rejoice.
>
> If in the dusk of the twilight,
> Dim be the region afar,
> Will not the deepening darkness,
> Brighten the glimmering star?
> Then when the night is upon us,
> Why should the heart sink away?
> When the dark midnight is over,
> Watch for the breaking of day.

Waiting—till the darkness is over, till the tempest is done. Watching—for the breaking of day, for the sunshine. Rejoicing in sorrow, listening for hope. It is patience that allows us to do this, patience planted and nourished by the Holy Spirit's presence in our lives.

---

One snowy afternoon my son brought home a picture from school. He had spent several days in art class drawing and coloring it. It was the typical "January picture": snowman in top hat, falling snow, solitary tree. It wasn't until several days later, as I looked at this magnet-hung scene on my refrigerator door, that I realized the tree had green leaves. There, in the middle of a winter white landscape, my son had placed a summer tree.

I asked him about it later, "Well," he replied, "even in winter, I see the trees with green leaves."

Vision. That's what patience is all about. Vision to see beyond the bleakness that surrounds us to the brightness of better days. Vision to see the possibilities and not just the problems in people. Vision to believe. Vision to *wait*. "The fruit of the Spirit is . . . patience."

# CHAPTER FIVE

*Wherever there is a human being there is an opportunity for a kindness.*

Seneca

# KINDNESS

*KINDNESS.* LIKE PANTALOONS OR "CAN-CAN" CRINOLINES, kindness seems a bit old-fashioned to many people. In our competitive society, kindness seems a quaint and sentimental carry over from simpler, slower days. In a push-and-shove world, few see the need to stop and pick up the casualties who are being trampled by the ambitious and the apathetic.

But kindness is still very much the fashion when it comes to pleasing God. It is a one-word summary of Jesus' whole philosophy of human relations: "In everything, do to others what you would have them do to you" (Matthew 7:12). Kindness is adorning yourself with the Golden Rule, bypassing the costume jewelry of the world for ornaments of gentleness and mercy.

Kindness means going beyond obligations—cheerfully. It means expecting nothing in return for your overtures and efforts. Kindness is saying, "God and I love you!" by giving up your seat on the bus, by visiting a sick neighbor, or by helping a new child find his or her way to Sunday school class. The nature of kindness is spontaneous and unconditional. Kind deeds need not be premeditated, thought through, or highly planned productions. More often they will be spur-of-the-moment bubblings, prompted by the Holy Spirit.

The apostle Paul tells us in Ephesians that, because of divine kindness, we have been adopted into the heavenly family: "And God raised us up with Christ and seated us with him in the heavenly realms in Christ Jesus, in order that in the coming ages he might show the incomparable riches of his grace, expressed in his kindness to us in Christ Jesus" (2:6-7). Kindness is grace displayed—on God's part and on ours. It is a willingness to do good for others. It is deliberate and voluntary and other oriented.

We are surrounded by daily reminders of God's benevolent nature—the soft rays of morning, the inviting coolness of summer twilights, the hymns of swallows and whippoorwills. Acts 14:17 says that God "has shown kindness by giving you rain from heaven and crops in their seasons." Rain restores moisture in and life to parched plants. Kindness can be a restorative, too, putting vitality into the drudgery of daily living and refreshing the limp spirit of the lonely.

Kindness embodies not only a compassionate, but also a forgiving, nature. We are called to "Be kind and compassionate to one another, forgiving each other, just as in Christ God forgave you. Be imitators of God" (Ephesians 4:32–5:1). Because we are God's children, we are called to be like our heavenly Father. We are commanded to imitate his forbearance and forgiveness.

My favorite poet is Emily Dickinson. Born on December 10, 1830, in Amherst, Massachusetts, she was a recluse and an avid observer of nature. Perhaps taking stock of her solitary life and its limited opportunities prompted Emily to pen this poem:

> If I can stop one heart from breaking
> I shall not live in vain;
> If I can ease one life the aching,
> Or cool one pain,
> Or help one fainting robin
> Into his nest again,
> I shall not live in vain.

How clearly she caught the true character of kindness, for kindness is not acts of flaunted philanthropy or deeds of meretricious grandeur. It is, rather, giving tender attention to the minute, the common, the unsung things of life.

My friend Nancy has a real talent for growing perennials. Every summer her yard bursts into bloom with peonies, miniature carnations, tiger lilies, and roses of every shade. Whatever the occasion, Nancy creates bouquets of extraordinary beauty. Last year, during my bout with pneumonia, she showed up with an armload of daisies. "To help you recuperate," she said.

And they did. Their perfect centers and creamy petals soothed my tired spirit. But despite daily vases of fresh water and careful trimming of crimped stems, the flowers began to wilt. Their heads hung forward; an air of resignation surrounded the once beautiful bouquet. They were dying. Soon the inevitable happened: I tossed them into my waste basket along with used Kleenex and read newspapers.

Often we Christians become enamored of "beauty"—spending money, expending energy, and investing time to perfect our outward appearance. Yet we strive in vain if we sever ourselves from our spiritual "roots." Just as cut flowers fade, so will our pretensions at outward comeliness without the inner confidence of Christ enthroned in our lives. First Peter 3:4 tells us that our attractiveness should be found in the "unfading beauty of a gentle and quiet spirit." Unlike creams and cosmetics, unlike designer suits and expensive haircuts, gentleness and kindness are always durable, desirable, and delightfully practical.

When I was a child, I had a Shetland pony named Sugar. I spent all my spare time currying her and riding her and leading her around the farm as I tended to my chores. Soon, Sugar followed me everywhere, even without a halter or rope. When I went inside for lunch, she would stand on the back porch with her nose pressed against the screen door. Those loving acts of kindness on my part had made Sugar loyal and eager to be with me.

Hosea, in speaking of God's care for his people, says that:

[God] led them with cords of human kindness,
  with ties of love;
[God] lifted the yoke from their neck
  and bent down to feed them.

Hosea 11:4

Just as Sugar was bound to me by "cords of kindness," so also are we drawn to God by his kindness to us. We are not forced to follow God by a tether that jerks us forward. We are, rather, beckoned by his gentle care.

We Christians are called to show that same kindness to the world. Our pull on them is not dogmatism or philosophy or churches with padded pews. It is kindness, kindness so gentle and genuine that even a push-and-shove world will stop and take notice.

I once knew a saintly old woman who spent her days and her strength doing for others. On a small card kept in her purse, she carried the words that had become the motto of her life: "Let my life be one of broken bread and poured out wine." That was her philosophy, and through the years hundreds of people had been touched by her acts of charity and sharing and kindness.

Christmas 1971: My husband had been drafted in 1970, and now, eighteen months and four states later, was assigned to Fort Riley, Kansas. Until then, my only connection with Kansas had been through Dorothy and Toto. Now I was to have a Kansas Christmas and a Kansas baby.

I pulled the collar of my worn wool coat tightly around my neck. The tattered vinyl belt barely reached around my bulging middle. Half-frozen droplets stung my cheeks and clung to my eyelashes as I hurried down the slushy Junction City sidewalk, splashing through murky puddles and floating chunks of gray snow.

The USO sign swayed in the December wind. Red, white, and blue stars had been painted on the front of the building, and the entrance wore a faded plastic wreath. Inside, the room smelled of space heaters and cigars. Two soldiers were playing checkers on a card table nearby. A warped ping pong table stood near the back wall. Rows of battered paperbacks, their covers mended with masking tape, were shelved along one side.

A weathered-faced soldier leaned lazily against the bookshelves, peeling an orange. The pungent citrus smell filled the dingy room. I leaned against the door frame and closed my eyes.

Suddenly, I was back home in Indiana, and Mother was baking her famous orange cakes for the Christmas festivities. A child again, I was pushing orange halves against the juicer, watching the golden liquid spill into the bowl. Outside, fresh snow whirled playfully, caressing fenceposts and silos. Birch trees, like virgin brides, boasted white on white. Pine trees posed for Christmas cards. Children's voices could be heard as young carolers made their way to our inviting front porch . . .

"Merry Christmas!" a voice rang out. Startled, I opened my eyes. My daydream faded, and I was abruptly back in the present. A small woman was peering into my face. "Say," she wanted to know, "are you all right?"

Standing erect, I managed a weak smile. "Guess I'm a little tired," I murmured.

The woman's name was Molly. "Here, let me take your coat," she said, as she hustled me toward a well-used, over stuffed chair. "How about a cup of peppermint tea? When is your baby due?" Somehow the concern in her voice made the worn upholstery of the chair feel friendly and more familiar.

While answering her businesslike questions I found myself stringing popcorn, testing lights, and searching through stacks of ancient record albums for Christmas music. When I next noticed the clock on the wall, a pleasant hour had slipped by.

I mumbled something about getting home before dark. As I was about to leave, Molly took my face between her gnarled hands. "You and your husband will eat Christmas dinner with us," she said. "We have turkey and all the trimmings." For an instant the idea repulsed me—a charity meal served on plastic trays. "We're family," Molly added, as though she sensed my feelings, "and it's Christmas." Then quickly, and with surprising strength, she hugged me.

Warmed both in body and soul, I began to walk toward the base and our quarters. Then I noticed that the sleet had turned to snow and huge, airy flakes floated around me. Already a sparkly film covered the ground. Christmas lights winked through wisps of white.

I stopped at the commissary. Gingerly, I handled the oranges, searching out the juiciest for the orange cakes I would make for the USO Christmas dinner.

"You certainly are particular," a friendly stranger smiled at me. "I bet you're baking a little something for your family."

"You're absolutely right," I beamed. Molly's hospitality had turned a shabby room into a sanctuary of understanding. Her warm concern had made her seem like kin, and her kindness had made me glad—for oranges and Christmas and Kansas.

---

Dorcas stood on her rooftop, watching the rays of morning walk across the choppy waves of the Great Sea.

Already the poor had begun moving about on the beach, looking for bits of rags or refuse that might wash ashore. Dorcas turned away, a sickening feeling welling up inside her as she remembered what had washed ashore yesterday: bodies. Two bloated bodies of shipwrecked sailors. It seemed as though she could still hear the screaming wails of the widows. Dorcas pushed the sounds from her head and started down the steps to her sewing room. Those widows and their children would be needing clothes, and they would come to her for help. The needy of Joppa always did.

The book of the Acts of the Apostles describes Dorcas as a disciple "who was always doing good and helping the poor" (9:36). She used her fingers and funds to sew cloaks and robes for the needy. A woman of substance, she chose to give not only her means, but also herself. Her kindness was known throughout the city, but she shunned notoriety, desiring to be consecrated rather than conspicuous.

Then a series of events made Dorcas very much the center of attention. First, she became ill. Friends gathered to care for her, but her condition quickly worsened and Dorcas died. While they washed her body and placed it in an upstairs room, the disciples sent word to Peter: "Please come at once!"

Peter came. He entered Dorcas' house and found it filled with mourners. "All the widows stood around him, crying and showing him the robes and other clothing that Dorcas had made while she was still with them" (9:39*b*). Peter put them all out of the room and, praying a prayer filled with Pentecostal power, commanded Dorcas, "Get up." She opened her eyes and sat up—a living, breathing miracle. Because of this wonder, many people in Joppa believed in the Lord.

What did Dorcas do then? Well, she didn't write a book

or begin an extended speaking tour. She didn't spend her afternoons signing autographs on the veranda. Instead, she threaded her needle and quietly began to sew, once more stitching shattered lives together with Christlike kindness.

---

In a log cabin in northern Pennsylvania on July 9, 1838, Philip Paul Bliss was born. Influenced by his musical and deeply religious father, Bliss later became a composer and song leader. It was while directing the singing for a series of meetings featuring lay preacher Dwight L. Moody that Bliss was inspired to write one of the great hymns of that era.

As he closed his message, Moody told the story of a captain who was attempting to bring his boat into the Cleveland harbor on a dark and stormy night. Beneath a starless sky, the ship was tossed by vicious, mountain-high waves. Clinging to the mast, the captain peered into the storm, searching for a signal light to guide the vessel to safety. He spotted a single light glimmering from a lighthouse set high on a rocky bluff.

He turned to his pilot and asked, "Are you sure this is Cleveland Harbor?"

"Quite sure, sir."

"Then where, in the name of heaven, are the lower lights?"

"Gone out, sir."

The captain's voice grew tight. "Can we make the harbor?"

"We must, sir," the frightened pilot replied, "or perish." In the darkness, the pilot missed the channel. The boat piled up on the rocks and settled to a watery grave.

Moody concluded this story with the statement, "Brethren, the Master will take care of the great lighthouse; let us keep the lower lights burning."

Philip Paul Bliss was deeply moved by the illustration. From its images and message, he wrote the gospel hymn "Let the Lower Lights Be Burning."

> Brightly beams our Father's mercy
> From His lighthouse evermore;
> But to us He gives the keeping
> Of the lights along the shore.
>
> *Refrain:*
> Let the lower lights be burning!
> Send a gleam across the wave!
> Some poor fainting, struggling seaman
> You may rescue, you may save.

Like that captain and pilot, many people today are groping in darkness. Our gentle deeds and heartfelt kindnesses are the "lower lights" that lead others to the Light.

---

When we are truly filled with the Holy Spirit and truly attentive to his gentle proddings, our simple acts of kindness can have surprising, and rewarding, effects. That's a lesson I learned when I bought a very special fabric remnant.

Unlike Dorcas, I do not sew. Buttons give me trouble; hems baffle me completely. So when I joined a "Work and Witness" team going to Honduras, I had difficulty knowing what "sewing piece goods" to take for the national pastor's wife, Santos. I persuaded my sister, the seamstress of the family, to accompany me to the fabric store and help me pick out something suitable. While Sis skimmed through the ginghams and polyesters with a practiced eye, I rummaged through the remnant table. My eye was soon taken by a large piece of heavy fabric. Its navy blue background was splashed with jaunty green parrots and fuchsia pink flowers. "I like this," I ventured.

"Be reasonable," my sister retorted. "It's too heavy for a dress, the pattern is too big, and it probably won't even make up nicely!"

I knew she was right. Yet, I was so drawn to that colorful piece of heavy cloth! So, while an Indiana snowstorm raged ouside the window of the fabric shop, I bought the bright remnant.

Once in Honduras, I began to feel foolish about my choice of fabric. It was so hot there! I knew that Santos would not want to wear anything made from that bulky cloth, and none of the houses had curtains. I couldn't imagine what possible use Santos would have for that hunk of heavy color. I chided myself for such impulse buying. Then came the day before our departure, the day I had to give Santos my gift.

Reluctantly, I handed her the wrapped package. I stared down at my sandals, feeling my cheeks flush. I listened as she slipped off the ribbon, removed the paper, and opened the box. Then there was silence. Such silence. I looked up into the face of Santos, unprepared for what I saw there.

She was crying! Quickly I took one end of the material and helped her spread it out on the kitchen floor, thinking perhaps she would like the fabric if she saw its pattern. Soon green birds and pink flowers lay in colorful display on the sprawled cloth.

To my dismay, she began to cry even harder. But she was laughing, too! She hugged me, as her words spilled out in a mixed muddle of English and Spanish.

"O *bonita!* Pretty! For my bed, *si?* I have never had—how you say—bedspread. But for long time now Santos pray here in her heart for bedspread. And you, my sister from far country, bring my bedspread! Glory *a Díos!* Praise God!"*

I laughed with Santos, while inside, my heart grew full with the simplicity of Santos' faith and with the reality of her answered prayer—a prayer I had helped to answer. It is through our offered kindnesses to one another that God uses us. Dorcas. Me. You. "The fruit of the Spirit is . . . kindness."

Adapted from *Hoosiers in Honduras* by Mary Lou Carney. Copyright © 1986 by Nazarene Publishing House.

---

# CHAPTER SIX

*A saint is one who makes goodness attractive.*
Laurence Housman

# GOODNESS

---

GOODNESS. NO OTHER QUALITY IS MORE CLOSELY ALIGNED with the character of God. When I was a child, my daily table grace began, "God is great; God is good. . . . " When I first memorized Psalm 23, I was powerfully moved by the image of "goodness" following me, everywhere and forever, "all the days of my life" (v. 6).

*Goodness* was Grandma's word for God, the term she used whenever any family crisis arose. "Let's hope to Goodness," Grandma'd say, "that it rains on that parched corn." Or as I helped set the table for Sunday dinner, she'd admonish, "In the name of Goodness, mind your manners when the reverend is here!" And when my sister and I played "Indian" and turned the back porch into a besieged fort, Grandma would put her hands to her ears and implore, "For Goodness' sake, stop that racket!"

As any elementary teacher can tell you, the suffix "ness" means "state of being." So, by definition, *goodness* is the "state of being good." But the question, "What is good?" has been discussed by philosophers, debated by politicians, and sermonized by religious leaders for centuries. Like many words that have been a part of our vocabulary since childhood, goodness is more complex than it appears.

Goodness is generosity. It begins with God's abundance bestowed to us—sunshine and laughter, seedtime and harvest, forgiveness and reconciliation. That divine generosity must, in turn, flow through us to our fellow creatures. Second Corinthians 9:10 promises us, "Now he who supplies seed to the sower and bread for food will also supply and increase your store of seed and will enlarge the harvest of your righteousness." God's generosity is sure. Verse 11 goes on to explain why we are recipients of this unmerited gift: "You will be made rich in every way so that you can be generous on every occasion, and . . . your generosity will result in thanksgiving to God."

A Christian's giving is purposeful giving, not done for the sake of notoriety or commendation, or even done consciously. It is generosity based on a desire to see God glorified, to see his likeness mirrored in our actions. Anne Morrow Lindbergh, in her book *Gift from the Sea,* talks about the nature of purposeful giving, saying "it belongs to that natural order of giving that seems to renew itself even in the act of depletion. The more one gives, the more one has to give—like milk in the breast." To be good is to be generous, with time as well as talent, with patience as well as pennies.

Goodness is honesty. As Christians, we must act responsibly, dealing with others in fair and candid ways. We have been called to renounce "secret and shameful ways," to be a people who "do not use deception" (II Corinthians 4:2). To live a life characterized by goodness means to be trustworthy and concerned with the rights of others. And it means adhering to the highest form of honesty—truthfulness of the soul, where façades are dropped and inadequacies laid bare at the feet of a loving Father.

Goodness is duty, acknowledging and accepting the fact that we have a responsibility to do God's work here on earth. Paul ends his letter to the Galatian church with an appeal to do good to everyone, to carry one another's burdens. "Let us not become weary in doing good, for at the proper time we will reap a harvest if we do not give up" (Galatians 6:9). *If*—the biggest little word in our language. If we persist in doing our duty, the harvest is assured. God's work truly is our work.

On a tombstone in Shrewsbury, England, are inscribed these words:

> For the Lord Jesus Christ's sake,
> Do all the good you can,
> To all the people you can,
> In all the ways you can,
> As long as you can.

Our duty is not simply to be good; it is to be good for something. "Therefore, as we have opportunity, let us do good to all people" (Galatians 6:10).

Goodness is virtue. It is the attaining of a moral excellence that holds firm in times of testing and temptation, during periods of conflict and concern. Virtue is integrity tried and proved.

During the rule of the Roman Empire, a foot soldier could conscript an ordinary citizen to carry his pack for one mile. At the end of that mile, the citizen was free to go his way. Christ told his followers, "If someone forces you to go one mile, go with him two miles" (Matthew 5:41). That's what virtue does. It sees what must be done—and does more. It knows what is required—and goes beyond. Virtue rises above the base requirements of "right" and "wrong" to become inherent goodness. It goes the second mile.

Goodness is righteousness. By very nature, humans are corrupt beings. "In Adam's fall, we sinned all," proclaimed an early primer. Righteousness cannot be gained through personal diligence or self-denial. It is not the result of initiative or insistence. "This righteousness from God comes through faith in Jesus Christ to all who believe" (Romans 3:22). It is only through the atoning sacrifice of Christ that goodness is possible. Through justification, we are made right with the law; through sanctification we are made like God. And God is *good*.

Goodness. It's the very fabric of Christianity, a fabric as serviceable as it is gracious, as wholesome as it is holy.

The gauge on my Oldsmobile diesel rested on the large, red "E." I knew I had to find fuel soon, but the interstate roads of upper Michigan were unfamiliar and sparsely populated. I decided to take the next exit and try to find a service station. I soon saw the welcome green and white sign that assured me there really was life lurking just out of sight of this endless asphalt. I exited, and sure enough, a service station stood just up the road. Its pumps, however, were rusty. Knee-high grass grew in what had once been a paved lot. Disgusted, I made a U-turn to head back for the highway.

It was then I noticed the house across the road, a white farm house almost hidden by a profusion of trees and bushes. There, in its graveled lane, was a "market" of sorts. A wooden crate was the table on which had been placed an old coffee can filled with fresh asparagus spears. Beside this was a smaller can. A large chalkboard leaned against the display. It proclaimed:

SELF SERVICE.
70¢ a bunch. Leave money in can.

I stared at the scene, at first amused and then awed by such an expression of trust. I could imagine some hardworking farm wife as she placed the box and fresh produce in the shade of the maples that lined the driveway. With hands more accustomed to crimping pie

77

shells than printing letters, she had written the sign. And then she had turned back to her chores, certain that people would, indeed, "Leave money in can."

Honesty expects honesty. Part of being good is anticipating that same behavior in other people; it is trusting higher motives and nobler actions to emerge. Goodness embodies an optimism born of goodwill.

When my daughter was going through the "terrible two" stage, days were often filled with tests of her will and my stamina. After one particularly difficult afternoon, I exiled her to a chair in the corner of the kitchen until she could, as I put it, "learn to behave."

As she sat rocking her doll, she looked up at me and sighed, "But Mommy, why don't you just *make* me be good?"

Goodness is a choice, a direct result of the indwelling presence of the Holy Spirit. God does not make us good. He provides us with the provision for righteousness, but he does not imprison us so that we become controlled creatures with no free will or self-direction. First Corinthians 10:13 says, "No temptation has seized you except what is common to man. And God is faithful; he will not let you be tempted beyond what you can bear. But when you are tempted, he will also provide a way out so that you can stand up under it." God enables, but we must deliberately turn from evil.

The story is told of a little girl whose aunt sent her a pin cushion for her birthday. Being a well-bred young lady, she wrote a thank-you note for the gift. It read:

> Dear Auntie,
>   Thank you for the birthday present. I have always
>   wanted a pin cushion. But not very much.

If we would bear the fruit of goodness, we must work for it. We must want it. Very much.

When we are truly filled with the goodness of God, we

are anxious to share that goodness with others. "Always be prepared to give an answer to everyone who asks you to give the reason for the hope that you have" (I Peter 3:15*b*). With Christ as Lord, we become not reluctant witnesses, but rather animated proof of God at work in our lives.

No image more vividly portrays the changed life of a Christian than that of darkness and light. "For you were once darkness, but now you are light in the Lord. Live as children of light (for the fruit of the light consists in all goodness, righteousness and truth) and find out what pleases the Lord" (Ephesians 5:8-10). This passage makes it clear that we were not in darkness; we were darkness. Now, through the gift of reclamation, we actually are light!

My house is the old-fashioned kind, with a long lane and lots of windows. Every year on the day after Thanksgiving, armed with extension cords and packages of orange Christmas bulbs, I begin the methodical placing of electric candles in all the windows. That night my family and I officially begin the Christmas season by plugging in every candle and turning off all the other lights. Then, bundled in layers of flannel and wool, we walk down our driveway. When we reach the main road, we turn to face our house.

Every window shouts with light. The tiny bulbs seem magnified a hundred times. That's the way it is with goodness. It shines in a world of selfishness and subversion. And its rays, magnified by God's might, touch even the darkest corners of human souls.

Medical science has proven that man's ability to see is determined by the length of light rays that strike the eye. That's why astronaut Gordon Cooper attested to seeing cars and trucks on the highways during his first orbital flight around the earth, even though he was one hundred miles away. In fact, our innate ability to see is limitless; it is the variable of light rays that lessens or enlarges vision.

Goodness, as well, is available in unlimited supply. We have only to open the eye of the soul and let the light of God flood our being. We will then learn the true meaning of *being good*, for we will sense the vision of God's work. And ours.

Being good means knowing what is truly important. When we bear his fruit, the Holy Spirit guides us past the looming importance of our own concerns to the quiet intensity of the needs around us.

I hardly noticed her as I tossed my books on the corner of the library table. I glanced at my watch; two whole hours were mine before I had to pick up my son from nursery school. I opened my books, scattered note cards on my half of the large oak table, and began my third reading of *Pilgrim's Progress*. That Western Traditions II class! All that stood between me and my master of arts degree was a final paper on Bunyan and his *Pilgrim's Progress*. I was having trouble getting started. Too many interruptions and too much indecision had brought the due date for my paper precariously close. I forced my attention to the book, trying to ignore the early spring sunshine that lay on the table in variegated patterns.

Sitting across from her, I could hear the scratching of her pencil—slow and unsure—as it moved across the sheet of typing paper. From the corner of my eye I glanced at her hand; gnarled knuckles awkwardly gripped the pencil. I tried to give Bunyan my full attention. I felt the table jiggle as she shifted her position. A deep sigh resonated from her direction. Promising myself only a quick glance, I looked up from my reading.

She was hunched over a large paperback book. Her thin gray hair was pinned tightly into a knot at the back of her head, but soft, gossamer strands fell toward her face like childish tendrils. She wore a cotton house dress of faded red print. The pencil paused; she looked up suddenly, and our eyes met. I had expected her eyes to be dim hazel or even ashen. But they were incredibly blue, a dancing blue that should have belonged to Santa Claus or to a birthday child or to a bride. She smiled. Before I could give her my please-don't-talk-to-me-I'm-busy-smile, she launched into conversation.

"You know, I never did understand this noun and verb stuff," she said, brushing a wisp of hair from her damp forehead. "How can anyone tell one from the other? They all just look like words to me." She laughed a timid laugh of frustration.

I looked into her face. Tiny wrinkles played around her eyes. Her mouth was pursed with determination; small beads of sweat stood on her upper lip. I pictured her in a large kitchen, expertly seeing to every detail of a fragrant holiday dinner. I imagined her cradling a sick child in the night, humming lullabies while bathing the tiny face with cool water. Then I saw her as she now sat across from me, bewildered by elementary facts that eluded her mind. Somehow my Bunyan paper seemed less important than it had when I hastily chose this table near the window. Unknowingly, this small, wizened lady had waved the one flag I couldn't ignore.

"Oh, I'd be glad to help you. I teach high school English. Let's see what you're doing." I slid out of my chair and into the one next to hers. Her face broke into a broad smile, alabaster white teeth that made her eyes seem even more blue.

"That would be good. My name is Mildred," she said simply.

"Now, Mildred," I began, remembering countless seventh-grade lessons on the parts of speech. "A noun names a person, place, thing, or idea. The things you see and touch—like this desk or pencil—are nouns. This library is a noun. The people in this room are nouns. Things that exist without concrete forms—like love, freedom, goodness—are nouns."

Mildred stared deeply into my eyes. A small crease formed in the middle of her high forehead. She savored my every word. I could have been explaining the mysteries of ancient Egypt. "Here, let me see your book so I'll know what you're supposed to do." She handed me the stapled book, which I recognized as the kind used by those studying for high-school equivalency tests.

As I scanned the grammar section of the book, Mildred talked freely. "I never could do English. My father was a mean man. He beat me with a razor strap till the blood came, but still I could not get English." There was no reproach in her voice, only a little sadness that time had not erased. "But I can do arithmetic. Add things in my head lickety-split. Not all that high school stuff, but long division is like a great, fun puzzle. I know how to make every part fit just so." She waved her small hand in the air, her index finger magically calculating some unseen problem of admirable difficulty.

"Looks like all eight parts of speech are included in your book," I interjected.

"I was sixteen when I finally made it to high school," she continued, oblivious to my remark about her grammar book and now lost in a world of long-ago memories. "But I made it to high school," she said, and for just a moment her hunched shoulders seemed erect. Then her eyes became overcast as she continued. "But I was an epileptic. I never had a seizure at school, but my English teacher, she didn't want me in the room with the other kids after she found out. Made me sit on the floor in the hall." She placed her wrinkled hand on my arm and, looking closely at me, repeated, "Made me sit on the floor in the hall. What kind of thing is that to do to Mildred, who worked so hard to get to high school!"

I listened in shocked disbelief, remembering Ron, who three times had seizures during my English class. I remembered the concern of the other students, the calm competence of the school nurse, and the small bundle of tongue depressors I kept in my desk. "And so, I left school." Mildred shrugged, gesturing with her palms up. "That was in '39. Now old Mildred tries to learn." When she looked at me then, her eyes were again that radiant, sparkling blue. "Ask me what a noun is," she said. And I did.

The hours passed quickly. I explained pronouns and verbs. Mildred interposed comments about her job at the nursing home and her dream of becoming a bookkeeper. Glancing at her watch, Mildred exclaimed, "Oh, my! I must be going. My daughter, she lets me do my wash at her house, and I have to go now." She slipped her arms into the green sweater that hung on the back of her chair. It was misshapen and nubby from many washings. She fumbled with the buttons.

Turning to me, she proudly put out her hand. I could feel her rough skin and calloused palm, firm and powerful in my own smooth grip. "Thank you. You are a nice person and one smart lady with them nouns and such."

I smiled. "You're more than welcome, Mildred."

As she gathered up her books to return them to the reference desk, she looked longingly at the pencil in her hand. It was obviously new, shiny red with a perfect eraser and a flawless point. "You know, I borrowed this from the lady at the desk. But I'm going to buy me some of these, some just this pretty. I can use them now that I'll be doing nouns and such." Mildred laughed, and this time the laugh was all confidence and determination.

After she left, I realized I had time only to gather my

things before leaving to pick up my son. As I stuffed the bare note cards inside my copy of *Pilgrim's Progress*, I smiled. I wasn't sure what dear Professor Scheimann of Western Traditions II would think about how I had spent my afternoon, but I somehow thought Bunyan—and Christ—would approve.*

---

Naaman stood beside his horse, feeling waves of anger and disappointment sweep over him. "How dare he!" Naaman shouted to Ammoni, his servant. "I come with rich gifts of silver and gold. With clothing as fine as any found in the king's palace!" Naaman looked at the heavily laden retinue, remembering the long trip from his own country of Syria. "Yet this so-called miracle worker denies me even the simple courtesy of seeing me. Instead, he sends his servant with that message, 'Go, wash yourself seven times in the Jordan.' Ha! Are not our rivers a thousand times cleaner than the detestable Jordan? *There* I shall bathe, but never here in this muddy water!"

As Naaman reached for the bridle, he looked at his hands and felt again the sharp pangs of realization. The leprosy was worsening. Mottled white patches covered his hands and forearms. He squeezed his eyes shut and fought back the fury and despair that filled his chest. "Am I, commander of the armies of Syria, to die the degrading death of a leper? Why, O God of Israel, why?"

Naaman mounted his horse for the long ride home. How hopeful he had been! What wonderful things he had heard about this Elisha! And he had come prepared to give rich gifts, to perform brave deeds. But to wash in the Jordan River! Perhaps the prophet had meant it as a joke or even an insult.

---

*Adapted from *Today's Christian Woman*. Nov./Dec., 1983. Used by permission.

"Forgive me for speaking out, Master," Ammoni began.

Naaman looked down into the face of his faithful servant.

"What is it, old friend?"

"If the prophet had told you to do some great thing, would you not have done it? If he had demanded payment of lands and livestock, would you not have given it? How much easier it will be to do as he requests, to wash yourself in the Jordan River seven times. It can do my master no harm."

Naaman smiled wryly. What did he have to lose? His dignity, maybe, but that seemed a small price to pay for the possibility of healing. And he had heard such wonderful things about the God of Israel and his prophet Elisha. Perhaps Ammoni was right.

The prophets of the Old Testament were a fiery bunch, spewing out "woes" on wayward kings and smashing the altars of false gods. Elisha stands out in this group as a man filled not only with the intensity of God's judgment, but also with the fullness of God's love.

It all began when Elijah summoned Elisha, who was plowing his father's fields. Elijah commissioned him to be his disciple. From that moment on, Elisha devoted himself to God's work. Soon, wrapped in the mantle of his predecessor, he began his ministry, a ministry that would span five decades and be marked by miracle after miracle. Wherever Elisha went, people recognized him as a "man of God." Not because he carried engraved calling cards asserting such. Not because his servant ran before him proclaiming such. Elisha's banner was goodness; it permeated his life and laid the foundation for his miracles. It marked him as a man of God.

From the very start of his calling, Elisha pleaded for a "double portion" of God's spirit. This burning hunger filled him with God's presence—and God's power, a power Elisha used to encourage the disheartened, to help the needy, and to convict the sinners. He spent his life among his neighbors, demonstrating practical compassion and resourceful responsiveness. Like the Messiah who was yet to come, Elisha "went about doing good."

What happened to Naaman? He took those murky dips in the Jordan, just as Elisha had told him to do, and "his flesh was restored and became clean like that of a young boy" (II Kings 5:14). He then returned to his own country, convinced that there was only one true God "in all the world" (v. 15).

Goodness. Now, as then, it is helpful and compassionate, pratical and holy, sensitive and responsive. Like Elisha, we are each one called to be instruments of God's will, to become vessels of God's goodness.

---

On an especially warm afternoon in June, 1851, Eliza Edmunds Hewitt was born. Her father's house was on a shaded Philadelphia street, and it was in that city she would spend her nearly seventy years. Eliza grew to be a bright and ambitious girl, one who loved working with children. Consequently, few people were surprised when she became a public school teacher. Every Sunday she taught Sunday school. She filled her life with the laughter of children and the wonder of learning.

But a painful spinal malady brought her teaching career to an abrupt end. Her days were now filled with pain and frustration. Feelings of inadequacy taunted her. Then Eliza began to study God's promises—to sincerely study them, searching for the answers and encouragement she so desperately needed. During the months of her semi-invalidism and slow recuperation, the thirty-six-year-old teacher struggled to know more about the wonderful work of her heavenly Father, to know more of the life and ministry of his Son.

To her amazement and joy, Eliza discovered that God had endowed her with the rare gift of being able to write simple, but beautiful, stanzas. In 1887, she penned the words that best expressed her hunger for a more meaningful walk with Christ. Later set to music, that poem became the beloved hymn "More About Jesus."

> More about Jesus would I know,
> More of His grace to others show;
> More of His saving fullness see,
> More of His love who died for me.
>
> More about Jesus let me learn,
> More of His holy will discern;
> Spirit of God, my Teacher be,
> Showing the things of Christ to me.
>
> More about Jesus in His Word,
> Holding communion with my Lord;
> Hearing His voice in ev'ry line,
> Making each faithful saying mine.
>
> More about Jesus on His throne,
> Riches in glory all His own;
> More of His kingdom's sure increase;
> More of His coming, Prince of Peace.

We will bear the fruit of goodness as we learn more about Jesus—as we absorb his thoughts and motives, as we learn to discern his will. Our goodness depends on our total allegiance to the cause of Christ, "for it is God who works in you to will and to act according to his good purpose" (Philippians 2:13).

----

I live in a small town in which summers are marked by specials at the root beer stand and library sponsored movies in the park every Friday night. The culmination of the season occurs late in August, when the Catholic church holds it annual festival, "A Taste of St. Pat's." Area restaurants compete to create culinary delights. On long tables beneath huge shade trees, they offer their wares: corn dogs and baklava, smoked pork and potato skins, chicken salad and blueberry muffins. For a nominal price, customers are given tastes of these treats. Almost everyone in town turns out for a day saturated with the aromas of barbecued ribs and fresh-baked breads, a day filled with the flavors of tasted specialties. When the festival is over, the participants load up their spits and spatulas and go back to their businesses, leaving us with just enough of a taste to want more. I have no doubt the restaurant business picks up considerably during the ensuing weeks.

Peter talks about a special kind of "taste festival" in his first epistle: "Like newborn babies, crave pure spiritual milk, so that by it you may grow up in your salvation, now that you have tasted that the Lord is good" (I Peter 2:2-3). We must "grow up" in our salvation. We must "taste" the Lord's goodness, and then go back for more. Until we are filled with the very essence of God. "The fruit of the Spirit is . . . goodness."

---

# CHAPTER SEVEN

*Faith is not belief in spite of evidence, but life in scorn of consequences.*

Elton Trueblood

# F A I T H F U L N E S S

---

*FAITHFULNESS.* THE YEAR WAS 1806, AND JOHN COLTER HAD left the Lewis and Clark expedition to strike out on his own. For months he hiked through scenes of extraordinary beauty, finally arriving in what is now Yellowstone National Park. The area was breathtaking, boasting volcanic plateaus surrounded by pine-covered mountains, crystal lakes, and—most amazing of all—geysers, one of which erupted with startling regularity. Colter took a faithful account of these wonders back to the settled regions of the United States, but the public refused to accept his amazing stories. It was decades later, convinced by a photographer and artist who visited the region, that Congress passed an act creating the first national park in the Yellowstone region. Today that same geyser John Colter saw continues to erupt, faithfully, every hour. And thousands of people each year come to see "Old Faithful."

Whether in natural phenomena or in next-door neighbors, faithfulness is an admirable virtue. In an age that indulges situational ethics and looks for legal loopholes to negate pledged agreements, faithfulness is in scant supply.

To be faithful means to be full of faith, to trust in God and in his promises. However, it also entails the determination to maintain a Christian commitment at any cost. Faithfulness is not a pale promise to try to live a "good" life. It is a fierce determination to be like Christ in an unChristlike world.

If we are to bear the fruit of faithfulness, we must not only believe in Christ, but also act on that belief. Faithfulness includes two kinds of faith: vertical and horizontal. Vertical faith is our loyalty to God; horizontal faith is our loyalty to one another. The former necessitates a full surrender, the latter a full commitment.

In writing to the church at Thessalonica, Paul compliments the members on their steadfastness. "We ought always to thank God for you, brothers, and rightly so, because your faith is growing more and more, and the love every one of you has for each other is increasing" (II Thessalonians 1:3). The Greek word for growing used in this passage really means "to grow *luxuriantly*." As our faith in God grows, so does our faithfulness to our fellow human beings.

As children of God, we are called to be faithful because "God . . . is faithful" (I Corinthians 1:9). We must be constant and sure to our promises, just as he is to his. We must be incorruptible in our actions and above reproach in our motives. To be faithful is to be reliable in every circumstance. Faithfulness makes us worthy of the confidence of others; it makes us comrades with God.

Faithfulness results in a determined Christian walk. It frees us from the ups and downs of indecision, from the vacillations of pretended devotion.

When it was time for me to learn to drive, my father took me to the middle of a pasture and put me behind the wheel of our old pick-up truck. As he talked me through the process of pushing in on the clutch and shifting gears and releasing the clutch while pressing on the gas—and what seemed like a thousand other impossible commands—I lurched the truck around the field. Often I would take my eyes off the windshield to struggle with the gear shift on the floor. During those times, I would swerve precariously close to the fence row before Dad called my attention to the approaching barbed wire and steel posts. But the lessons continued week after week, until one day my father said, "How about driving me to the mailbox?" Smiling, I turned confidently onto our gravel lane.

In Hebrews, Paul issues a call to Christians to persevere, to be steadfast: "Let us draw near to God with a sincere heart in full assurance of faith. . . . Let us hold unswervingly to the hope we profess, for he who promised is faithful" (10:22-23). *Unswervingly*—that's the essence of faithfulness. I learned to drive that truck in a straight and sure path only when I learned to keep my eyes on what was ahead. It's the same with our faith. We can only be consistent and effective Christians when we keep our eyes on the "hope we profess" and not on the circumstances that oppress and frustrate us.

Samuel Taylor Coleridge was the youngest of fourteen children and received his education at a charity school in London late in the eighteenth century. He is best remembered for his poetic masterpiece *The Rime of the Ancient Mariner*. This epic poem is a fascinating tale about a ship and its crew who are lost in a land of ice and fearful sounds. When hope is almost gone, a great sea bird, an albatross, appears through the fog and mist, bringing with it a strong south wind that moves the ship out of danger. But the ancient mariner, without provocation, shoots the bird with his crossbow. The fortunes of the ship again take a turn for the worse, and the crew hangs the dead albatross around the neck of the ancient mariner as a symbol of his guilt. The rest of the story is a tale of supernatural woes, until at last only the mariner is left alive.

Proverbs 3:3 admonishes

> Let love and faithfulness never leave you;
> bind them around your neck,
> write them on the tablet of your heart.

Just as the albatross was a symbol of the mariner's guilt, so also our faithfulness is a symbol of our reconciliation to and our new life in Christ. The mariner was never free from the influence of his encumbrance; so we, too, will be affected by the persistent presence of faithfulness. Our lives will be characterized by allegiance to the cause of Christ. The albatross hung from his neck as a reminder of willfulness and impetuosity. Faithfulness must be bound to us as a reminder of the true nature of God and of the expectations placed on us as his children.

If our lives are not filled with faithfulness, they will be filled with deceit and disloyalty. In Hosea, God brings a charge against his people, Israel: "There is no faithfulness, no love, no acknowledgment of God in the land" (4:1). A lack of faithfulness is always accompanied by other sins—love of self, denial of God. Unless we are truly faithful, we leave ourselves open to the subtle and subversive influence of Satan. If our commitment to Christ is one of simple convenience, one that wavers with the first winds of opposition, then we are still bound by sinful nature.

> The acts of sinful nature are obvious: sexual immorality, impurity and debauchery; idolatry and witchcraft; hatred, discord, jealousy, fits of rage, selfish ambition, dissensions, factions and envy; drunkenness, orgies, and the like. I warn you, as I did before, that those who live like this will not inherit the kingdom of God. (Galatians 5:19-20).

We cannot claim Christian attributes while wading in the quagmire of faithless living.

A few years ago, one of the families in our church lost everything when their lovely brick home burned to the ground. They moved to a temporary rental home while the children finished out the school year, and they began the heartbreaking job of sifting through the charred remnants of their possessions—the ashes of family albums and childhood mementos. Yet, they did not surrender to despair. Later, the mother told me that one of the few salvageable things she found in the ruins was her Bible. "As I picked it up," she said, "I realized that God wanted me to concentrate on what was left, not on what was lost. We had each other; we had our faith. That was enough."

Suffering offers us a chance to demonstrate the quality of our faithfulness to God. Job, in the midst of his sufferings, proclaimed the wisdom of God:

> But he knows the way that I take;
>   when he has tested me,
> I will come forth as gold.
>
> Job 23:10

Our trials are the purifying fires that forge a faithfulness more valuable than gold.

When I was a child, I watched for hours as my grandmother made patchwork quilts. She would sort through the big basket of cast-off fabric scraps, matching colors and textures to create just the design she wanted. Often I would recognize pieces—the pink of an Easter dress long-forgotten, blue print from my sister's favorite skirt, a patch of purple flowers that used to be a pocket on Mother's apron. Then she carefully cut each one, using a pattern made from newspaper print. Every night, after chores were done, I would find Grandma "piecing" those bits of cloth, faithfully creating quilts that would layer me in colorful warmth all through the cold winter nights. As she sewed, she told me about her life in the hills of

Kentucky, about how she was saved in a tent revival meeting, and about how much she was looking forward to seeing her sister Ida in heaven.

Several of those quilts are mine, now. Their colors are faded and their edges frayed, but they're still beautiful. Whenever I open the cedar chest and finger their delicate stitches, I am reminded again of Grandma's faithfulness—in the way she worked and in the way she lived. And I pray for the courage to be like her.

When my husband and I bought our first home, the shrubs in front of the house had not been trimmed in years. Their branches were big and sprawling, their tops shapeless and broad. They grew almost gutter-high, obscuring the view from both the living room and the bedroom windows. We tried to cut them back, to shape them, to somehow make them again ornamental instead of atrocious, but it was no use. At last we pulled them out and replanted with small evergreens, promising to trim them faithfully.

In our lives, it's easy to let grievances and differences, snide comments and half-truths take root and grow. Unchecked, they soon spread their thorny branches across the windows of our souls, obscuring the Son and leaving us in the damp darkness of nurtured hurts. True faithfulness allows us to weed out those things that would come between us and God; it commits us to daily diligence in living a Christian life.

Hebrews 11:1 gives us the classic definition of faith: "Now faith is being sure of what we hope for and certain of what we do not see." *Sure. Certain.* To bear the fruit of faithfulness means to be so filled with faith that there is no room for doubt.

For weeks I had been troubled by a situation that seemed hopeless. My prayers had gone unanswered. My expectancy had turned to despair. Then one evening, as I was hurrying to clean the kitchen before leaving for a meeting, the electricity went out. Our house sank into a twilight stillness as the lights and radio ceased to work. I retrieved a book of matches from the top of the stove and lit the kerosene lamp that sat on a nearby shelf. Bringing it close to the sink, I continued to scrape our dinner plates and load them into the dishwasher. My son watched for a few minutes and then said, "Too bad the dishwasher won't work anymore." I smiled, realizing how silly it must look to him—my loading an electric dishwasher by kerosene lamp light. Then I explained to him that the outage was only temporary, that the electricity would come on again soon.

In that moment, I realized the essence of faith is believing—truly believing—in those unseen, hoped-for things in life—things like returning electricity. And answered prayers.

I am always moved when, via the media, I am able to witness the inauguration of the president. The mood is solemn because the business at hand excludes levity. The newly elected president places his hand on the Bible and repeats: "I do solemnly swear that I will faithfully execute the office of president of the United States. . . ." From that moment on, he assumes the rights and the responsibilities of the highest office in the land. Twenty-four hours a day, every day, he is president. He must honor his oath to be faithful in doing everything possible to protect and defend all that is best about our country.

Being a Christian is a full-time job, too. We are called to be like our Father, who is "the faithful God, keeping his covenant of love to a thousand generations of those who love him and keep his commands" (Deuteronomy 7:9). Through the Holy Spirit's indwelling, we are called into communion with God. We are elevated to the station of divine heirs with Christ. Our oath to follow him, to be his ambassadors to a sinful world, must be taken with great seriousness. We are not called to flit and fritter our days away; we are called to bear the fruit of faithfulness.

---

Joshua pushed back the flap of his tent and looked into the valley. Sun rays glinted off rocky ridges, flooding the hills with shafts of golden light. Joshua sighed. This morning, every joint in his body ached! These last seven years of conquest in Canaan had been victorious, but vigorous. And Joshua was tired. For over eight decades he had seen God faithfully fulfill his promises to his people. Now he was finishing his final job: allotting the land to the tribes, as the Lord had commanded through Moses. "And perhaps then," Joshua whispered to wisps of clouds high overhead, "I shall rest with my fathers."

"Joshua, I would speak with you."

Joshua turned to see Caleb's tall figure silhouetted against the brightness. "Then let us sit in the morning sun and talk, old friend. My bones cry out for warmth."

The two settled in front of the tent. Caleb, like Joshua, had seen many years, but his white hair and beard seemed to make his eyes even brighter, and his broad shoulders were strong and erect. "You remember our days together," he began, "days of revelry and sadness, days of plunder and mourning."

Joshua nodded. "I remember it all."

"And you know how you and I spied out the land for Moses, how we brought back grapes and figs the like of which had never before been seen."

"And even then my blood stirred to go up and take the land," Joshua said, "to claim the wonder of God's plan for us."

"Now, after these many years, all has come to pass as God promised, as Moses said." Caleb paused to look at the valley below, drenched in sunlight and dew. "We have come into the promised land—the land flowing with milk and honey, the land we urged our brothers to enter forty years ago. So now, Joshua, in keeping with what Moses promised me on that day, grant me my inheritance." Caleb shook his fist toward Hebron, the very land he had spied out many years before. "I am as strong this day as I was on that day Moses sent me. Together the Lord and I shall drive out those pagan giants who made our brothers shiver with fear! I shall avenge the cowardice of Israel fourfold." He laid his hand on Joshua's arm. "Give me this mountain!"

The scene is not unfamiliar. Two senior citizens sitting in the warmth of the morning sun—except for one thing. Caleb was not simply reminiscing. He was preparing to battle the fiercest men in all Canaan; he was claiming a right he had earned through forty years of watchful waiting and faithful service.

The story of the children of Israel and their exodus from Egypt is a powerful one, filled with strong characters, such as Moses and Aaron and Joshua. But throughout the narrative, Caleb stands as the man who did not succumb to the pressure of peers or the perils of impatience.

Years before, as Moses and the Israelites first neared Canaan, the people became fearful about what they would find waiting for them there. Would they be slaughtered by the inhabitants? Would their wives and children be sold as slaves? Would they all be taken into bondage and forced to work for cruel taskmasters as had their fathers before them? To assure the people of the good land that awaited them, the Lord told Moses to send men to explore the land, one man from each of the twelve tribes of Israel.

For forty days, these men explored Canaan, finding at every turn bounty and beauty, just as the Lord promised. Finally they came to the Valley of Eshcol, where lush grapevines hung heavy with clusters so great it took two men to carry samples of the fruit back to camp! But the land was not without challenges. Its occupants were city dwellers, men of might. When the spies returned to give their report, it was this fact—of fortified cities and giants— that colored their descriptions. Ten of the twelve talked only of the fearful inhabitants, the impossibility of conquest.

But "Caleb silenced the people before Moses and said, 'We should go up and take possession of the land, for we can certainly do it' " (Numbers 13:30). He and Joshua stood firm in that opinion, certain that the Lord, who had delivered them from the land of Pharaoh, the God who had given them manna and quail, would not desert them now.

> The land we passed through and explored is exceedingly good. If the LORD is pleased with us, he will lead us into that land, a land flowing with milk and honey, and will give it to us. Only do not rebel against the LORD and do not be afraid of the people of the land, because we will swallow them up. Their protection is gone, but the LORD is with us. Do not be afraid of them. (Numbers 14:7-9)

The people, however, chose to believe the cowardly spies. In their anger to silence Caleb and Joshua, they picked up stones to kill them. But God was not far from his faithful followers, and his glory appeared with a blinding brightness that brought the whole assembly to their knees.

But the damage had been done; the wrath of the Lord burned against the weakness and wickedness of Israel. He swore that not one man who had seen his miraculous signs done in Egypt and *en route* to the promised land would live to set foot in Canaan. A whole generation would wander in the desolation of this unclaimed promise; desert winds would swirl sand across their graves. "But because my servant Caleb has a different spirit and follows me wholeheartedly, I will bring him into the land he went to, and his descendants will inherit it" (Numbers 14:24).

The next day all the people turned back toward the Red Sea.

New Moon festivals passed; Sabbaths came and went. One by one, the generation of unbelievers died. Only Joshua and Caleb remained, remnants of those who had seen the mighty steeds of Pharaoh swallowed by the Red Sea, who had known the cloud of God's presence, who had tasted the sweetness of water as it gushed from that desert rock. A new generation, nourished on the Lord's commandments, came of age. It was this generation that followed the battle cry of Joshua as city walls fell before them and mighty warriors fled in dread of the God of Israel.

The word *caleb* means "bold." Perhaps that's a good synonym for *faithful*, because faithfulness demands a dogged allegiance, an unwavering commitment. Throughout this account, the word *wholeheartedly* is used repeatedly to describe Caleb's devotion to God. He was as certain of God's power and providence at eighty-five as he had been at forty. He was as sure of his commitment the day he asked Joshua for his inheritance as he had been the day the crowd tried to stone him.

Faithfulness is not without its rewards, "but the way of the unfaithful is hard" (Proverbs 13:15). The ten spies who brought back the pessimistic report have long since sunk into oblivion. But Caleb and Joshua live on as heroes. Joshua did give Caleb his "mountain," and in the name of the Lord, Caleb conquered every obstacle, establishing a land for his family for generations to come. Now, as then, the faithful of God are blessed with God's presence in this life and his assurance of glories yet to come.

The fruit Caleb helped carry back from Canaan was impressive. But the fruit he displayed during those long years in the desert, during those fierce years of conquest, was just as impressive. It's a fruit we can bear, too, in the tedium of daily routine, in the trauma of tested belief. It's a fruit Caleb knew sprouted in patience, grew with diligence, and basked in the brightness of God-inspired optimism. It's the fruit of faithfulness. The God of Caleb waits to bring it to maturity in us, too.

---

The Reverend William Orcutt Cushing was a powerful preacher who served well his New England parish, but he was forced to surrender his pulpit when he suddenly lost his power of speech. Knowing that without voice he was useless as a minister, he struggled to find God's purpose in this calamity. Faithfully he prayed, believing that God would give him another avenue of service, trusting that some special task awaited his doing. His lips formed the words as day after day he prayed in his heart, "O Lord, give me something to do for thee!"

The answer came in an unexpected way, for God gave Mr. Cushing the gift of writing songs and sacred hymns. It was a talent he never knew he possessed, a career he had never dreamed of attempting. The songs that flowed from his pen were filled with the fluid recounting of God's faithfulness and love.

Perhaps Mr. Cushing is best remembered for his hymn "Follow On." The piece was inspired by Psalm 23:4, "Yea, though I walk through the valley of the shadow of death, I will fear no evil: for thou art with me" (KJV). The lyrics are an autobiographical account of Cushing's struggles through months of readjustment.

Down in the valley with my Saviour I would go,
Where the flow'rs are blooming and the sweet waters flow.
Ev'rywhere He leads me I would follow, follow on,
Walking in His footsteps till the crown be won.

*Refrain:*
Follow! follow! I will follow Jesus!
Anywhere, ev'rywhere, I would follow on!
Follow! follow! I will follow Jesus!
Ev'rywhere He leads me I will follow on!

Down in the valley with my Saviour I would go,
Where the storms are sweeping and the dark waters flow.
With His hand to lead me I will never, never fear;
Danger cannot fright me if my Lord is near,

Down in the valley or upon the mountain steep,
Close beside my Saviour would my soul ever keep.
He will lead me safely in the path that He has trod,
Up to where they gather on the hills of God.

Faithfulness is following our Savior—anywhere, everywhere, always. It is knowing the fellowship of the Holy Spirit in our hearts and the smile of God on our lives. Faithfulness is living the Christian life in spite of the fluctuations and temptations that surround us. It is "walking in His footsteps till the crown be won."

---

I first heard the story in prayer meeting one Wednesday night. The pastor asked for volunteers to recall times when God had been especially faithful to them. Alma stood to speak, her silver hair neatly waved, her eyes bright behind her bifocals.

"It was when my babies were little," she began. "We were living in a tiny cottage on Jefferson Street, back an alley behind a big, white house. Bill was working every day, but he only made about fifteen dollars a week—and that didn't go far, what with rent and food and two little ones. But we watched our pennies and tithed and got along fine. Until it came time to buy new license plates for our automobile.

"I remember the plates cost nine dollars, and we plain didn't have it. So when it came time to buy new ones, we just had to stop driving the car. Now Bill walked to work. It was a long way, but he had to do it. The people he worked for let him drive one of their trucks home for lunch, but we had no way to get to church. It was too far to walk. I wanted for my young'uns to be in Sunday school, and I missed the services so! But there was no money for license plates. So I began to pray. Every day. I wasn't sure what to pray for. I just told God how much we wanted to go back to church and figured he could think of some way to make that possible.

"Well, one morning, after Bill had set off for work, I got this terrible burden for our problem. I prayed and prayed about it. I tried to think of how to make the money, but nine dollars was a big amount back then! I prayed all morning. When Bill turned in the alley at noon, I saw him get out of his truck and pick up something. He came into the kitchen with the biggest grin on his face, waving a brand new ten dollar bill."

Alma stopped here, to wipe her eyes with a corner of her hanky. There were a few other moist eyes, too, including mine.

Faithfulness. It's our response to the faithfulness of God. It's our rebuttal to a world seeking self-gratification.

Someone of lesser faith might have wondered where

that ten dollar bill had come from. But Alma knew. God had put it there so she and her little girls could go to church. What about the extra dollar that was left after buying the nine-dollar license plates? Alma tithed it, of course. "The fruit of the Spirit is . . . faithfulness."

---

# CHAPTER EIGHT

*There is nothing truly great but lowliness.*
François Fénelon

# GENTLENESS

---

GENTLENESS. IT'S A TRAIT AS MUCH MALIGNED AS IT IS underrated. My favorite musical is Lerner and Loewe's *Camelot*. Set in the imaginary (and idyllic) kingdom of Camelot, the story is a spirited retelling of the legend of King Arthur and his colorful subjects. Its music captures the many moods of that medieval age, from revelry to reverence, from pageantry to pathos. One song, titled "The Seven Deadly Virtues," is sung by a bawdy group of knights who find the virtues extolled by the church to be a bit too demanding. One line of that song asserts, "It's not the earth the meek inherit, it's the dirt!" That's a sadly accurate summary of the view today's society has of meekness. To many people, to be gentle is to be weak; to be humble is to be spineless. In a system that idolizes power and spends millions every year on assertiveness training, gentleness seems as archaic as the customs of King Arthur's court. Yet, we as Christians are told repeatedly to "be completely humble and gentle" (Ephesians 4:2). Does this mean we must live without rights, being pushed and prostrated by our more aggressive counterparts? What, really, is Christian gentleness?

Gentleness is deliberate kindness in dealing with others. It is a quiet courtesy that colors our interactions with neighbors, co-workers, strangers, and family alike.

Christian meekness is voluntary thoughtfulness; it is nonviolence made rich because of its holy origin. Believers adopt a submissive spirit not out of cowardice, but rather "out of reverence for Christ" (Ephesians 5:21). Anne Ortlund, in her book *Disciplines of the Beautiful Woman,* says, "Never think that meekness is weakness. Meekness is strength under control." Gentleness does not preclude masculinity or ambition or self-confidence; it simply means these things have been put into their proper perspective, the perspective Christ lived and Paul taught in the New Testament.

Throughout his ministry, Christ constantly portrayed the role of gentle savior and healer. He who had "all authority in heaven and on earth" (Matthew 28:18) did not use that authority to call down lightning on the heads of hypocrites or to fill with sand the wells of his opponents. He outwitted those Pharisees who tried to trick him with questions about the law; he silenced the Sadducees with a wisdom they could only wonder about. Christ was as uncompromising as he was noncombative.

When he looked at the multitudes who followed him, Christ was filled with compassion, with a yearning urgency that they understand his person and his mission. He called them to him with the words: "Come to me, all you who are weary and burdened, and I will give you rest. Take my yoke upon you and learn from me, for I am gentle and humble in heart, and you will find rest for your souls. For my yoke is easy and my burden is light" (Matthew 11:28-30). The "yoke" was a familiar image to these common folk. The fields of Palestine were tilled by oxen joined together with heavy wooden yokes, dragging awkward plows. The multitude knew of other yokes, too—the yokes of slavery and servitude. The Romans laid heavy burdens of taxation and allegiance on the people they conquered; the Sanhedrin filled their lives with a thousand weighting details that made righteousness a frustrating impossibility. Then came Christ—offering a new way, one in keeping with his gentle, humble heart. His "burden" would not be legalism; it would be love. His "yoke" would not be subjection and servitude; it would be reconciliation and divine adoption.

Again and again Christ addressed the idea of humility. He condemned the Pharisees for their arrogance, for loving "the place of honor at banquets and the most important seats in the synagogues" (Matthew 23:6). Even his own disciples struggled with pride. In quelling a dispute among them about who should sit on his right and left hands, Jesus said, "The Son of man came not to be served but to serve" (Matthew 20:28 RSV). Later, he gave demonstration to those words when he washed their feet. God's own Son donned the towel of a servant to teach his disciples, and us, a much-needed lesson: Greatness is service.

Albert Schweitzer once said, "The only ones among you who will be really happy are those who will have sought and found how to serve." Ambition, money, success, notoriety—none will bring happiness unless the vital element of humble service is included. The gentle person is not one without initiative or intelligence. Quite the contrary, the gentle person is one who has found the wisdom of fearing God, who has learned that "humility comes before honor" (Proverbs 15:33).

In his letter to the Christians in Rome, Paul warned against conceit. His fear was that these new believers in Christ would begin to take pride in their spiritual and moral progress. He urged them, instead, to offer themselves "as living sacrifices, holy and pleasing to God" (Romans 12:1). With Christ's death, the system of animal sacrifices offered by priests was replaced by a religion based on total, daily commitment and personal responsibility. Paul goes on to say, "Do not conform any longer to the pattern of this world, but be transformed by the renewing of your mind" (12:2). In our day, as in Paul's, the church must be *different*. Unlike the push-and-shove, me-first attitude that pervades society, we Christians are called to renew our minds by remembering the example of Christ, by adopting his meekness, and by accepting his mission.

Paul's imperative in Romans 12:3 goes to the heart of the matter: "Do not think of yourself more highly than you ought." There is a difference between humility and self-castigation. Someone once said that humility is an honest assessment of our worth through God's eyes. We are all sinners, saved through the unmerited grace of God. We are all lumps of clay, given life and purpose through the breath of his being. We are nothing made something, not by our own efforts "so that no one can boast" (Ephesians 2:9). The fruit of gentleness gives us proper perspective. We neither overestimate nor underestimate our worth. We acknowledge ourselves as vessels and instruments; we present ourselves to be filled and to be used.

Alexander Pope was one of the greatest of eighteenth-century English poets. Many of his statements have the rare quality of being both pithy and profound, such as the following excerpt from his *Essay on Criticism:*

> A little learning is a dangerous thing;
> Drink deep, or taste not the Pierian spring:
> There shallow drafts intoxicate the brain,
> And drinking largely sobers us again.

I first came across these words in a high school literature book. Beside the first line, someone had written in the margin, "So go to school and live dangerously!" It wasn't until I was finishing my undergraduate work and was assigned to read the piece again that I understood what Pope was saying. A little learning may tempt one to brag and flaunt one's knowledge, but a truly educated person realizes how much more there is yet to learn. As my professor put it, "The more you know, the more you know you don't know."

It's that way with gentleness, too. If we feign meekness, forcing ourselves to be amiable and submissive, we may soon begin to glory in how disciplined we are, in how well we control our anger. We may take pride in the very acts that resemble humility. But if we truly bear the fruit of gentleness, the Holy Spirit is at work in us. We do not pretend to be forbearing with the faults and insults of others; we *are* forbearing because we realize that we ourselves are subject to the same falterings as those around us. A deep drink of humility is, indeed, sobering, for since the Son of God himself was meek, what right have we to be otherwise?

In his Sermon on the Mount, Jesus urged the people to "let your light shine before men, that they may see your good deeds and praise your Father in heaven" (Matthew 5:16). The "shining" Christ advocated here is not an ostentatious display of good-deed-doing. It is not a suggestion that the people sound trumpets to call attention to their acts of mercy. It is, rather, an injunction against feeling ashamed of being Christlike. It is an imperative to stand up and be noticed because of the lives we live.

James 3:13 says, "Who is wise and understanding among you? Let him show it by his good life, by deeds done in the humility that comes from wisdom." As new creatures in Christ, we are called to exercise a wisdom that is other-worldly, a wisdom characterized by humility. "But the wisdom that comes from heaven is first of all pure; then peace loving, considerate, submissive, full of mercy and good fruit, impartial and sincere" (3:17). Considerate, submissive, full of mercy—it's a wisdom that precludes pride and embraces the true foundation of holiness: humility.

The last part of Exodus 15 tells the story of the waters of Marah. Moses and the people had successfully crossed the Red Sea, escaping from their long bondage in Egypt. For three days they traveled in the Desert of Shur without finding water. When they finally came to Marah, they were desperate with thirst, but the waters were bitter. Neither man nor beast could stomach the acrid taste. So Moses cried out to the Lord, who showed him a piece of wood. When Moses threw that wood into the water, the water became sweet, and all the people drank their fill.

Gentleness is like that wood. Into a bitter, strife-filled situation it comes, bringing with it a peace and a sweetness that ripple to the frayed edges of confrontation. "A gentle answer turns away wrath" (Proverbs 15:1), and it sweetens situations as seemingly hopeless as were those bitter waters of Marah.

Nonverbal communication, or "body language" as it is sometimes called, is an integral part of the way people express their ideas and emotions. In addition to what we say with our verbal language, we are constantly communicating our real feelings and attitudes through our nonverbal clues—eye behavior, facial expressions, hand gestures. Philippians 4:5 tells us to "let your gentleness be evident to all." What a person "says" through posture, dress, and behavior may be a more accurate reflection of his or her attitude than are the words he or she speaks. We are not to talk about humility; we are to live humbly. We are not to lecture others on the necessity of meekness; we are to be meek. The Spirit-filled Christian is surrounded by an aura of gentleness that speaks louder than anything he or she could say. When a Christian does open his or her mouth to answer those who may criticize or misunderstand, the Christian does it "with gentleness and respect, keeping a clear conscience" (I Peter 3:16). Verbally and nonverbally, the language of the Holy Spirit is gentleness.

Several years ago, I went to Honduras with a group from my church. There, in the small mountain village of Danli, we constructed a block church for a local congregation. Next to the building site grew a poinsettia, a poinsettia *tree!* Its branches, boasting huge red flowers, arched over the roof beams of the new church.

Since my experience with poinsettias had been limited to the greenhouse variety, I was fascinated. In my faltering Spanish, I told one of the nationals that I had a poinsettia on the table in my house at home. His eyes widened in disbelief, but before I could explain, he hurried down the street. Soon he returnd with several other Hondurans. He wanted me to tell them about my poinsettia. I tried to explain that my plant was very small. They could not grasp this. They could only express awe that my house was so *big!*

Philippians 2:5-7 says,

> Your attitude should be the same as that of Christ Jesus:
> Who, being in very nature God,
>     did not consider equality with God
>         something to be grasped,
> but made himself nothing,
>     taking the very nature of a servant.

It was difficult for my Honduran friends, accustomed to towering poinsettias, to understand my table-top plant. So, too, it is difficult for us mortals to understand why Christ, omnipotent and eternal, chose to come to earth as a vulnerable man. We, who spend our efforts struggling to be something, cannot imagine One who willingly "made himself nothing." It is only with the help of the Holy Spirit that our finite, ambitious minds can grasp the concept of the incarnation. It is only through his indwelling that our attitudes can "be the same as that of Christ Jesus."

The big department store in our area mall has a yearly shoe sale that is *fantastic*. Bargain connoisseurs from miles around converge for this event. On the day of the sale, hundreds of pairs of name-brand shoes are marked down 40, 50, even 60 percent. Then, on the second day of the sale, a new incentive is added: a package deal of "buy one, get one free." After selecting a pair of shoes for purchase, you then get a pair of equal or less value absolutely free. A circus-like atmosphere prevails as we all wander around with our arms full of shoes and our faces full of smiles.

The Bible talks about some "package deals," too.

When pride comes, then comes disgrace,
    but with humility comes wisdom.

Proverbs 11:2

Pride and disgrace. The two are linked in a desperate cause and effect relationship, for egotism and self-sufficiency lead inevitably to ruin and dishonor. "But with humility comes wisdom"—what a blessed pair! An acknowledgment of our own inadequacies, of our own need for divine assistance leads directly to wisdom. Buy one, get one—the cost of humility is high because it involves a total surrender of self. But the rewards are great, because the acquired wisdom will be a composite of virtue and knowledge and the fear of the Lord. Wisdom is a bonus "more precious than rubies" (Proverbs 8:11).

François Fénelon was the Archbishop of Cambrai

from 1695 to 1715. Born into the aristocracy of France, he was educated in the finest schools. He was scarcely into his teens when it became apparent to all that he was, indeed, a brilliant young man. His background and intelligence, joined with his dedication to God, made him a great "director of souls" to many of the upper class. Despite his accomplishments, however, François Fénelon was noted for his humility and love. In a meditation closing his discourse, titled "Meet Ill Treatment with Humility and Silence," he says this:

There is no true and constant gentleness without humility; while we are so fond of ourselves, we are easily offended with others. Let us be persuaded that nothing is due to us, and then nothing will disturb us. Let us often think of our own infirmities, and we shall become indulgent toward those of others.

Spirit-guided gentleness lets us "often think of our own infirmities" rather than boast of our own accomplishments.

When I was a freshman, I was easily swept up in the flurry of my first college homecoming. Parades and games and concerts and plays—all were a welcome swirl of excitement. Especially important was the final evening of the weekend, featuring a formal banquet. I dressed carefully for my date that night, admiring the new lace blouse and long, rich velvet skirt I had bought for the occasion. With a final squirt of hair spray and a final swish of mouthwash, I left my dorm room to meet my date downstairs. He was waiting for me in the dorm's formal lounge, a sunken room filled with purple velvet chairs and, tonight, with elegantly dressed people. I paused on the top step, sure of myself and smiling at the admiring looks of several gentlemen. Then, without warning, my foot slipped. I chugged my way down the steps, landing in a crumpled, humiliated hump at the bottom. My shoe heel was broken, my skirt seam ripped. Hair pins hit the carpet with dull tinks, and I could feel a run in my nylons snaking its way up my leg.

The next morning, when I started down the hall for class, I noticed someone had copied Proverbs 16:18 in big letters and left it on my door:

> Pride goes before destruction,
>     a haughty spirit before a fall.

I'm sure at the time I saw little humor in the ribbing. My pride was still too bruised from my grand entrance the night before. But I have often thought about that verse since then—when I'm tempted to be just a little too pleased with myself, when I'm tempted to belittle the efforts of others. Most of our "falls" are not literal ones. Instead, they're the kind that leave us emotionally and spiritually jolted, the kind that shake us rudely from the complacency of self-esteem. Unless we allow the Holy Spirit to tame our "haughty spirit," those falls can be very humbling.

---

The smell of morning drifted up from the dewy field. On the horizon, a haze hung in lingering shades of gray. Jonathan pulled an arrow from his quiver. His hands shook as he again remembered the anger of his father, Saul, the night before. Why must it be this way? What had David done to make Saul want to kill him? Jonathan knew David crouched somewhere nearby, waiting for the promised signal, waiting to know if he could return, or if he must flee for his life. The *brrrringg* of arrows pierced the quietness of dawn. Three times Jonathan shot.

"Shall I get them for you, Master?" The young servant boy looked up into Jonathan's face.

"Yes, lad. Go fetch them." The boy ran toward the rock beside which Jonathan's arrows had landed. As he neared the spot, Jonathan called out, "Quickly, boy, the arrows are beyond you." It was the signal he and David had agreed upon, the sign that would tell David it was not safe to return.

The boy, wondering at the intensity of his usually gentle master, grabbed the three arrows and hurried back to Jonathan. "Here, Master," he said breathlessly. "I came as fast as I could!"

"You have done well," Jonathan said, mussing the boy's hair. "Now take my things back to the palace. I won't be long."

As soon as the servant had gone, David came from his place of hiding and bowed down before Jonathan. "Oh, my friend!" he cried. "What have I done to your father to make him hate me so? What is my crime?"

Jonathan pulled David to his feet. "You have done nothing! My father is mad with jealousy, for he knows that you will someday be king. Our friendship angers him, too. Last night he cursed me, telling me I am a disgrace to the kingdom. He insisted that I bring you to him, saying that only your death would establish my right as the future king of Israel."

"That much is true," David said sadly. "If I live, you cannot be king."

"What do I care about being king!" Jonathan yelled, pacing in the wet grass. "God has chosen to tear the kingdom from my father and give it to you. So be it. Only *live,* my dear friend. Live!"

The warriors faced each other, their eyes downcast and their throats tight with emotion. Then in a sweep of powerful arms, they hugged.

*114*

"Oh, Jonathan," David sobbed. "Must it end this way?"

Jonathan wiped his eyes with the back of his hand. "Go, David. Quickly. My father is not to be trusted. We have sworn our friendship to each other in the name of the Lord, and nothing can change that. Be strong, old friend. You will surely be king over Israel, despite the evil plans of my father. And when your kingdom is come, remember me!"

"Always! Our friendship shall be stronger than death itself!"

Then, with a final embrace, the two parted. Jonathan's sandals made dull, empty thuds on the road as he walked back into town to face his father, Saul. On the opposite side of the field, David ran through morning mist—heading for the wilderness, hoping to find a hiding place in the hills near the Salt Sea.

David and Jonathan. The story of their friendship is one of the most moving in the entire Bible. From the moment David emerged on the scene, as the slayer of the mighty Goliath, Jonathan was drawn to him. And David returned his admiration and respect and love.

During David's rise to power, Jonathan showed more wisdom than did his father the king. Unlike Saul, Jonathan was not jealous of David. A mighty warrior in his own right, Jonathan could easily have taken offense at this "upstart" from Bethlehem. But from the very beginning, Jonathan's gentle spirit was evident. He did not compete with David for the praises of the crowd or for the right of wearing the crown. Why? It certainly wasn't because he lacked courage! First Samuel 14 tells the story of how Jonathan and his armor bearer broke through Philistine lines, killing twenty men in hand-to-hand combat and causing enough panic that Israel was able to rout her enemies. Jonathan explained his seemingly rash plan of action this way, "Nothing can hinder the LORD from saving, whether by many or by few" (14:6).

That was his philosophy when it came to David and the kingship of Israel, too. He realized that David was God's anointed and refused to let his own pride get in the way of accepting that fact. Jonathan knew that, by rights, he should succeed his father as king, but he also knew it would be wrong to oppose God's chosen. So Jonathan made a truly meek decision: He decided it was better to suffer wrong than to do wrong. He not only refused to harm David, but also loved David "as he loved himself" (I Samuel 20:17).

Jonathan's dealings with David were marked by magnanimous gentleness, by deliberate submission. Jonathan exercised forbearance with his father, showing respect even while differing from Saul's actions. Jonathan's willingness to surrender all claims to the throne proved that his meekness was no mere pretense. He knew the importance of abasing himself so that, through another, God's plan might be accomplished.

Jonathan was a man who was submissive but not servile, meek but not sheepish. He was loyal to his friend, patient with his father, and true to himself. He was a man of controlled temperament and keen insight, one whose gentle courage bore quiet testimony to his noble character.

Along with two of his brothers and his father, Jonathan died on Mt. Gilboa while fighting the Philistines. David mourned his loss in a moving lament:

> How the mighty have fallen in battle!
>   Jonathan lies slain on your heights.
> I grieve for you, Jonathan my brother;
>   you were very dear to me.
> Your love for me was wonderful,
>   more wonderful than that of
>     women.
>
> II Samuel 1:25-26

For David, Jonathan was a faithful friend and a trusted ally. For us, Jonathan is an example of selfless surrender and of uncomplaining compliance with the will of God.

---

In the college town of Albion, Michigan, stands a three-story white clapboard house, home of the Delta Tau Delta fraternity. On the front lawn is a bronze sign, erected by the Historical Commission of Michigan, designating this spot as Registered Site #215. The plaque reads: "THE OLD RUGGED CROSS, one of the world's best loved hymns, was composed here in 1912 by Rev. George Bennard (1873–1958)."

George Bennard was born the son of an Ohio Coal miner. At the age of fifteen, he went to work in the coal mines to help support his widowed mother and his five brothers and sisters. Later, he joined the Salvation Army, in which he served God faithfully for fifteen years. Then, in 1910, he resigned his post to begin independent evangelistic campaigns and to devote himself to writing hymns and sacred songs.

Bennard was prolific in his composing, having written the words and music of over three hundred hymns. One of those hymns is the much-loved "The Old Rugged Cross." He explained the inspiration for the classic hymn this way:

> I was praying for a full understanding of the cross, and its plan in Christianity. I read and studied and prayed. . . . It was like seeing John 3:16 leave the printed page, take form and act out the meaning of redemption. While watching this scene with the mind's eye, the theme of the song came to me, and with it, the melody.

Perhaps no other song in the history of the church has achieved as much fame as has this one. It is a moving summation of the Christian faith.

On a hill far away stood an old rugged Cross,
The emblem of suff'ring and shame;
And I love that old Cross, where the dearest and best
For a world of lost sinners was slain.

Oh, the old rugged Cross, so despised by the world,
Has a wondrous attraction for me;
For the dear lamb of God left His glory above
To bear it to dark Calvary.

*Refrain:*
So I'll cherish the old rugged Cross,
Till my trophies at last I lay down.
I will cling to the old rugged Cross,
And exchange it someday for a crown.

The cross of Jesus Christ truly does have a "wondrous attraction" for Christians—an attraction the world cannot understand. What a powerful statement Christianity makes to the gilded and glittered of the world! At its very basis is a simple, wooden cross. An appropriate symbol, for nothing portrays more acutely the humility of Christ, who was

> led like a lamb to the slaughter,
>     and as a sheep before her shearers is silent,
>     so he did not open his mouth.
>
> Isaiah 53:7

The meekness of Christ peaked at the cross. It was his greatest sacrifice: innocence swallowed up by sin, gentleness ravaged by savagery. Christ's humble obedience initiated the plan of salvation; our humble obedience completes it.

"The Old Rugged Cross" appeals to people in all walks of life because of its simplicity. As Christians, our appeal to a lost, power-crazed world must be simplicity, too—a simplicity marked by a Christlike gentleness and humility.

---

It was an old school building, one whose vaulting hallway arches and steep stairwells made it more ornamental than functional. Elementary classes filled every room. Special classes—such as remedial reading, enrichment for the gifted and talented, special education, and classes for the hearing impaired—were housed in improvised spaces created by dividers and old lockers. Finally, there was no other choice than to turn the teacher's lounge into a classroom. So the faculty found themselves evicted to the old stage—an area noted for its abundance of heat in the spring and its lack of the same during winter months. But the teachers were undaunted. They fixed up the stage, creating paper "windows" to give them a perpetual view of summer. Since there was no clock, they made a paper "Simplex" that always read 3:15. They even had a cardboard fireplace with a pretend fire, for coziness, if not warmth. Furniture was crowded on the stage, looking like leftover props from long-ago plays. The focal point for the whole thing was a huge, hand-painted sign that said, "Life Can Be a Humbling Experience. Smile!"

Life in the Spirit is, indeed, humbling. With the gift of sanctification comes a clearer perspective of self-worth, of individual importance. Haughty insistence on having one's own way becomes submissive obedience. With the Holy Spirit's indwelling, we are made like Christ, in all his gentleness. Self is crucified, daily, so that true humility can result. Jesus said, "Whoever exalts himself will be humbled, and whoever humbles himself will be exalted" (Matthew 23:12). Self-importance and pomposity flaunt their way through life, inviting criticism and jealousy and abasement. But Spirit-prompted gentleness provides opportunities for earthly service and promises of eternal rewards. "Humble yourselves before the Lord, and he will lift you up" (James 4:10).

Life can be a humbling experience—a blessedly humbling experience. Smile! "The fruit of the Spirit is . . . gentleness."

# CHAPTER NINE

*Whatever weakens your reason, impairs the tenderness of your conscience, obscures your sense of God, or takes away the relish of spiritual things; in short, whatever increases the strength and authority of your body over your mind—that thing is sin to you.*
Susannah Wesley

# SELF-CONTROL

SELF-CONTROL. IN THE KING JAMES VERSION OF THE BIBLE, this fruit is called "temperance," a word whose strongest implications are against the evils of alcohol. I can remember being taken as a little girl to hear "temperance speakers" at the tent revival meetings held every summer. These speakers were fiery and eloquent as they expounded on the wickedness of wine and the sinfulness of strong drink. As I sat on that rough bench, stubbing my toe in the sawdust that covered the floor, I wondered what this had to do with Mama, Grandma, my sister, or me. Looking around, I wondered why the preachers were telling any of us this. The whole congregation looked plenty respectable! I wondered why they didn't put their suit jackets back on and take their message down to the local "beer joint," where they would find a much needier, if less receptive, audience.

It wasn't until years later, in retrospect, that I realized part of the reason those sessions were so popular with the regular church-going population was that they could go and listen—and feel self-righteous. They were abstainers; for most of them, liquor wasn't even much of a temptation. So proverbial pats-on-the-back were passed around during those temperance meetings, and the good folk left feeling that they were producing admirable quantities of the fruit of temperance.

But self-control—well, that's another consideration. Yet it's the consideration we, as Christians, must make. The fruit of self-control involves more than teetotalism; it involves moderation and self-restraint in many areas of life.

Self-control is the ability to control oneself—one's actions, feelings, and responses. Its presence means that an individual has assumed command over the body, that one has established authority over the natural appetites. A self-controlled person has learned to hold passions in check, to curb impulsive actions. It is a habitual self-restraint, not just a sporadic show of moderation. In the Christian sense, self-control is asserting divine intents rather than succumbing to base instincts.

Self-control is possible only to the extent that the sinful nature of humans is subdued. The Bible speaks repeatedly of "crucifying" the sinful nature and with it the passions and desires that lead to eternal destruction. "For we know that our old self was crucified with him so that the body of sin might be done away with, that we should no longer be slaves to sin" (Romans 6:6). It is through this process of elimination by extermination that we are freed from the rule of sin. It is through putting to death the carnal desires that we bring to life the joy of being Spirit-led. When we have expelled from our hearts the love of earthly passions, we become fit vessels for the Holy Spirit's fruit. "Put to death, therefore, whatever belongs to your earthly nature: sexual immorality, impurity, lust, evil desires and greed, which is idolatry" (Colossians 3:5).

Into the space created when we rid ourselves of self-indulgence comes a welcome replacement: the will of God. Carnality cannot abide alongside God's will. Each is mutually exclusive; each demands complete control.

Therefore, a Christian must "not live the rest of his earthly life for evil human desires, but rather for the will of God" (I Peter 4:2). Self-control includes a constant guarding against sensuality and fleshly indulgence.

Rooted in the Holy Spirit, self-control brings into our lives a fresh awareness of stewardship. Cleared of the clutter of self, we realize that we must make an accounting to God for our labor, our lives, and our love. Christ becomes the norm for measuring values, for modeling actions. Resourcefulness and integrity replace the debauchery of sinful indulgence. New life in Christ results in changed conduct, for one becomes "a new creation; the old has gone, the new has come!" (II Corinthians 5:17).

That self-control embodies the spirit and not just the letter of the law is made evident in Christ's warnings against adultery in Matthew 5:27-30. "But I tell you that anyone who looks at a woman lustfully has already committed adultery with her in his heart" (v. 28). The old injunction against adultery under the Mosaic law is incomplete. Christ brings new life, new insights, and new responsibilities. Desiring another's mate is as much against God's purpose as seducing another's mate. References to eliminating offending members of the body that might cause sin—gouging out an eye or cutting off a hand—vividly emphasize that complete self-control of the body is essential. It is only then that we can be filled with the presence and mind of God. Nothing short of total self-control is expected, and demanded, of those who would be part of God's kingdom.

The self-controlled life is one characterized by contentment rather than striving. When the passions and ambitions of the flesh are subdued, a sense of satisfaction with life as it is emerges. Paul wrote to the church at Phillipi: "I have learned to be content whatever the circumstances. I know what it is to be in need, and I know what it is to have plenty. I have learned the secret of being content in any and every situation, whether well fed or hungry, whether living in plenty or in want" (Philippians 4:11-12). What was Paul's "secret of being content"? It was surrendering self-importance; it was abandoning personal rights to champion the rights of others. It was claiming the assurance that "I can do everything through him who gives me strength" (v. 13).

With the control of the body comes a control of the spirit as well. When Nebuchadnezzar, king of Babylon, besieged Jerusalem, he carried off captives, one of whom would figure prominently in events to come. His name was Daniel. Selected for training and groomed for royal service, Daniel and his companions faced many challenges and temptations in the strange and glittering world of ancient Babylonia. Yet they determined to be true to God and to their religious commitments—even in the midst of flagrant idolatry and limitless royal power.

The first chapter of the book of Daniel recounts the story of Daniel's self-control when it came to feasting on the king's delicacies and imbibing the king's wine. "But Daniel resolved not to defile himself with the royal food and wine, and he asked the chief official for permission not to defile himself this way" (1:8). Note the spirit of the resolve. Daniel's abstinence was not a haughty display of superiority; it was not an act of open rebellion. Daniel asked the chief official for permission to refuse the food and wine. The graciousness of Daniel's entreaty attested to its sincerity. His ego was as firmly under control as was his stomach. No discipline is holy if it results in feelings of superiority. A truly self-disciplined person will assume no affectations of evil—or good. Self-control must include the control of one's spirit.

Every ancient city was surrounded by walls, many of

them twenty to thirty feet thick. Built of stone or rock or even sun-baked brick, these walls were of utilitarian rather than aesthetic design. Their purpose was protection from wandering marauders and advancing enemies. During times of danger, people living in the surrounding farmlands would flee to safety inside the cities. These walls were carefully built and maintained, for without them a city left itself vulnerable to the whims and ambitions of passing rogues and neighboring kingdoms.

Proverbs 25:28 tells us

> Like a city whose walls are broken down
> is a man who lacks self-control.

Without self-control, we are defenseless against the onslaughts of lust and passion. Like an unwalled city, the undisciplined person has no strength to withstand attacks, and the forces of Satan find such a person easy prey. It is only through the rigors of self-control that walls of truth and moderation are built. It is only through the mastery of self by the Master's plan that salvation is sure. Self-control is a defense system that must be carefully built, carefully maintained.

Colossians 3:1-2 admonishes us, "Since, then, you have been raised with Christ, set your hearts on things above, where Christ is seated at the right hand of God. Set your minds on things above, not on earthly things." How can we, as Christians, "set our hearts on things above"? It is only through self-control, through discipline fueled by divine strength. It is only through an assertive investigation of our lives and a dedicated surrender of ourselves that we can become like Christ. Several areas of life bear close scrutiny when it comes to self-control.

A Christian must exercise control over his temper. This is no easy task, because it includes not only controlling the expression of temper, but also actually curbing the cause of temper itself. "Better . . . a man who controls his temper than one who takes a city" (Proverbs 16:32). A Christian cannot dismiss temper with a casual, "Oh, I'm just highstrung." Life in the Spirit has no place for outbursts of anger, seething resentments, or spontaneous irritability. Acknowledging our own fallibility frees us from the burden of always having to be right, always wanting things our own way. It cures the cause of temper—carnality.

A Christian must have self-control over his or her own mind. Just as we train our bodies to keep them physically fit, so also must we train our minds to keep them spiritually fit. First Peter 1:13 says, "Prepare your minds for action; be self-controlled." In my son's elementary school, the cafeteria has a big poster hanging over its main entrance. The poster features the four basic food groups and, in big letters across the top, says You Are What You Eat. If what we feed our stomachs is important, how much more so is what we feed our minds! We are what we read and watch and think about and listen to.

A few years ago, the Lord began dealing with me about the type of music I was listening to. I really enjoyed rock and roll. Not heavy metal or punk rock bedlam, but what radio disc jockeys classify as "soft rock." I listened as I drove my car, cooked my meals, and cleaned my house. I bought an occasional tape of my favorite rock artist. It seemed a harmless diversion. However, at the Holy Spirit's prompting, I became aware of how often those lyrics drifted through my mind, of how often I found myself humming a tune whose sentiments were less than Christian.

Then the youth minister of our church began a seminar on rock and roll music. Defensively, I went, and the proddings turned to conviction. I knew I had to give up my rock and roll, but was unenthusiastic about what I thought to be the alternatives. So I changed the buttons on my radio and put my tapes in the neighbor's garage sale. And waited to be miserable. Instead, I discovered contemporary Christian music and a group of artists dedicated to serving God and not just selling albums. Now, I smile when a line from one of their songs ripples across my mind, and I silently offer it as praise to the God we both serve.

Rock and roll music, soap operas, popular romances, Sunday football games. Only you and the Holy Spirit know what things may be subtly undermining the spiritual training of your mind for the cause of Christ. I have copied Philippians 4:8 onto folded index cards, placing one on top of my television, one near my bookcase, and another beside my stereo. "Whatever is true, whatever is noble, whatever is right, whatever is pure, whatever is lovely, whatever is admirable—if anything is excellent or praiseworthy—think about such things." These little scripture reminders help me to remember that my mind is in training. And they help me avoid the "junk food" that will keep me from having "the mind of Christ" (I Corinthians 2:16).

I am a trivia enthusiast. I enjoy reading those totally irrelevant, but completely fascinating, facts. As our family was playing a trivia game one night, my son read the question on the card: "What is the strongest muscle in the body?"

I thought of pictures I had seen of weight lifters. I considered their bulging biceps and taut abdomens. Which muscle was strongest? And then I knew. "The tongue," I said confidently. And I was right.

To be Spirit-filled is to be in control of that feisty body member, the tongue. "If anyone considers himself religious and yet does not keep a tight rein on his tongue, he deceives himself and his religion is worthless" (James 1:26). In his chastisement of the Pharisees, Christ criticized them for worrying so much about what went into the mouth and so little about what came out of it. Christians must control their speech.

One summer I went on an overnight campout with a group from our local YMCA. As we hiked deep into the pine forest that skirts the edges of the Y property, sun filtered through the fluffy tops of the trees. "All right," Dave, our leader, began. "Stack your gear over by that tree and spread out in groups of two to find firewood. And not just big logs, either! We need other kinds of fuel, too. Look for tender kindling—tiny twigs like this." Bending down, he picked up several frail pieces, no thicker than toothpicks. "And we'll need some this size, too," he said, holding up a stick the size of a pencil.

When we had all reassembled with our armloads of wood, Dave carefully laid the fire. First, he arranged three logs in an *H* fashion and then began placing the tiny twigs at an angle on the middle log. When all was ready, he laid a single match to the wood, and it burst into flame.

Proverbs 26:20 says,

> Without wood a fire goes out;
> without gossip a quarrel dies down.

I learned something important from watching Dave build that fire. It's not just the big pieces of wood that create the flames; it's the twigs that really fuel the fire. That's the way it is with gossip, too. It's not enough that we, as Christians, refrain from slander and malicious attacks on the reputations of others. We must control ourselves so that we don't indulge in even a passing innuendo or a caustic comment. We must discipline ourselves to withhold even the smallest remark that might fuel the flames of gossip or that might spark misunderstanding.

I once heard an evangelist say that whenever the Bible issued an injunction not to do something, it also implied a responsibility to do the opposite of the forbidden thing. It's not enough for a Christian to bridle the tongue and refrain from gossip. The Christian must use the tongue for purposes of praise and admonition. Ephesians 4:29 gives us both sides of our responsibility: "Do not let any unwholesome talk come out of your mouths, but only what is helpful for building others up according to their needs, that it may benefit those who listen." With self-control, the strongest muscle in our bodies can also be our strongest witness for Christ.

The pastor's text that morning was Matthew 6:24: "No one can serve two masters. Either he will hate the one and love the other, or he will be devoted to the one and despise the other. You cannot serve both God and Money." I only half-listened as he began his message. I'd heard a hundred sermons on the evils of money, but sermons about the dangers of wealth were for the wealthy. So I thought, instead, about my sons's tennis shoes. He needed a new pair—again—and I felt that knot in my stomach as I remembered the price the orthodontist had quoted me for my daughter's braces. Then there was the washer—it was making grating, threatening noises that hinted of imminent and permanent disability. Hoard money? I couldn't even keep up with my bills!

Suddenly I was caught by something the pastor was saying. "Sometimes those who have the least money love it the most." It was a totally new idea to me, the possibility of having a consuming love for something one didn't have.

Christ's warning against greed, against becoming entangled in the luxuries and trappings of earthly life, is not just for the rich; it's for us all. We must exercise self-restraint when bombarded by radio and television commercials, each one trying to convince us we really *need* the advertised item. We must stand firm against the accumulation of goods that will sweep us into material-ism—and debt. We must heed the advice given us in Hebrews 13:5:

> Keep your lives free from the love of money and be content
> with what you have, because God has said,
>   "Never will I leave you;
>   never will I forsake you."

A Christian must exercise self-control over time. Ephesians 5:15-16 tells us that we must "walk circum-spectly, not as fools, but as wise, redeeming the time, because the days are evil" (KJV). *Redeem* means literally "to buy back." Time has a way of slipping past us, leaving undone our lists of resolutions and unaccomplished our well-thought-out goals. A thousand diversions wait to gobble our leisure minutes; a hundred thousand jobs clamor for our working hours. Bearing the fruit of self-control means learning to prioritize, as well as to economize, time. It is only through holy devotion and self-discipline that we can "redeem" the time given us.

The work ethic runs strong in Christians; it always has. Christ was a carpenter, Luke a doctor, Paul a tentmaker. The Bible stresses the importance of work, warning against "the bread of idleness" (Proverbs 31:27) and promising that "he who loves pleasure will become poor" (Proverbs 21:17). Charles Kingsley, in his book *Town and Country Sermons*, says,

> Thank God every morning when you get up that you have
> something to do that day which must be done, whether
> you like it or not. Being forced to work and forced to do
> your best will breed in you temperance and self-control,
> diligence and strength of will, cheerfulness and content,
> and a hundred virtues which the idle never know.

In this age of stress and burn-out and over-achieving, it is important that Christians recognize the importance of leisure and rest, too. Self-control for many means not so much committing themselves to work as it means weaning themselves *from* work. We limit God when we assume he is not in our merrymaking as surely as he is in our labors. Recreation really can be a time of "recreation," a time for renewing ourselves with fresh air or family or simple solitude.

Being self-controlled means making time for the truly important things in life, personally as well as professionally. When you monitor your activities at the Holy Spirit's leading, you will not only be "redeeming" your time, but you'll also be heeding Paul's advice in I Corinthians 10:31: "Whatever you do, do it all for the glory of God."

At the core of self-control is curbing the fleshly desires that so easily strangle life in the Spirit. Our day-to-day existence must be spent among those for whom self-gratification and worldly pleasures are the norm. Greed, casual sex, gluttony, alcoholism, pornography— all are their daily fair. Self-control demands that "as aliens and strangers in the world" we "abstain from sinful desires, which war against [the] soul" (I Peter 2:11). Christ's coming was not only to fulfill the law, but also to replace it with a more excellent way. The law could deal only with infractions; its substance was punitive. But regeneration brings with it a preventive element—the indwelling of the Holy Spirit. By his presence we are able to "put to death the misdeeds of the body" (Romans 8:13).

Henry David Thoreau was a nineteenth-century philosopher-writer who devoted his life to plain living and deep thinking. One of his statements, perhaps his best-known, hangs in a black metal frame above my desk. "If a man does not keep pace with his companions, perhaps it is because he hears a different drummer. Let him step to the music which he hears, however measured or far away" (*Walden*).

As a Christian, you will often feel "out of step" with those around you. It may seem that everybody is cheating on income taxes or watching R-rated movies on home videos or sleeping in on Sunday mornings. The easy thing is for you to become like them, to mimic their indulgent life styles. But listen in the quietness of your own heart and you will hear it: the drumbeat of the Holy Spirit. Don't step to the rhythm of the world, urging you into a life of carnality and emptiness. March, instead, to the steady *thrump* of the Spirit, calling you to a life of fullness and joy in the Lord. "Do you not know that your body is a temple of the Holy Spirit, who is in you, whom you have received from God? You are not your own; you were bought at a price. Therefore honor God with your body" (I Corinthians 6:19-20).

---

Esther watched from the palace window as the last fingers of night faded from the sky. Soon it would be time. "Great Jehovah," she whispered, "let the king be in a merciful mood!" Esther heard the sound of sandals on the pavement and looked down to see her cousin Mordecai coming into the courtyard. Dressed in sackcloth, he continued to mourn the plight of his people. "*My* people," Esther thought. Mordecai looked toward the window, and their eyes met. Esther seemed to hear again the words he had spoken to her three days before, when Haman's evil plot to kill all Jews had been discovered: "Who knows but perhaps you have come to the kingdom for just such a time as this."

Esther turned from the window and called her maids. "Come! Prepare me, for today I shall go to the king!"

The story of Esther is a fascinating one, featuring a "rags to riches" beginning, a middle filled with villany and courage, and a "happily-ever-after" ending. But at the heart of the story stands a woman whose modesty and self-control, whose dedication and discipline determined the fate of the entire Jewish population living in Persia during the reign of King Xerxes.

A Jewish orphan, Esther was brought by her cousin Mordecai to the palace after Queen Vashti had been deposed. Together with other virgins selected from throughout the kingdom, she began a twelve-month beauty program that would prepare her for her one night with the king. Then, unless the king was especially impressed with her and asked for her by name, Esther would become simply another of his concubines.

From the moment of her arrival at the palace Susa, Esther found favor with those around her. Hegai, who was in charge of the "contestants" for the queenship, liked her at once. Not only was Esther lovely, but also there was a quiet strength about her, a modesty and shyness lacking in the others. Immediately Hegai provided Esther with everything she needed, including seven maids and the best place in the harem. But Esther would not allow the splendor of court life to overwhelm her. The vanity of her competitors repulsed her. Strengthened by a strong relationship with God, she resisted the sensual idol worship that flourished around her.

One by one the girls were called into the king, and one by one they were assigned to the place of the concubines. When Esther's turn came, she humbly trusted Hegai to tell her what to wear and what to take. She then went to King Xerxes with dignity and assurance, confident that God's will would be done, knowing that God's will was best. And "the king was attracted to Esther more than any of the other women, and she won his favor and approval more than any of the other virgins. So he set a royal crown on her head and made her queen instead of Vashti" (Esther 2:17).

Time passed, and onto the scene came Haman, hater of Mordecai, who tricked King Xerxes into signing a death sentence for all Jews throughout the kingdom. This was a crisis to which Esther must respond, for to remain silent meant sentencing her people to certain death. However, intercession on their behalf would not be easy, because Esther had not been summoned into the king's presence for over a month. To approach the throne uninvited carried with it the death penalty—unless the king chose to hold out his golden scepter in mercy. King Xerxes was not noted for his mercy.

So how did Esther prepare for her fateful meeting with the king? Did she wear a new silk robe? Did she have more beauty treatments? Did she try a high-protein diet? No. She told Mordecai, "Go, gather together all the Jews who are in Susa, and fast for me. Do not eat or drink for three days, night or day. I and my maids will fast as you do. When this is done, I will go to the king, even though it is against the law. And if I perish, I perish" (Esther 4:15-16). Esther met this crisis not with self-indulgence and vanity, but with discipline and courage—and faith.

God honored Esther's prayers; he had respect for the fasting of his people. When Esther approached the king, "he was pleased with her and held out to her the gold scepter that was in his hand" (5:2). He offered to give her anything she requested, "even up to half the kingdom" (v. 3). Ever cautious, Esther realized that she was dealing with sinister forces who wielded both power and wealth. She proceeded carefully, preparing banquets for the king and Haaman, biding her time and biting her tongue until the time was right.

Then Esther told the king of Haman's plot to kill her and all her people. King Xerxes, in his anger, hanged

Haman and gave his vast estate to Esther, who promptly bestowed those riches on Mordecai. What was to have been a day of slaughter for the Jews became, instead, a day of celebration. So completely reversed were the circumstances that "many people of other nationalities became Jews because fear of the Jews had seized them" (8:17).

Esther. Her behavior two dozen centuries ago in faraway Persia is our example of one whose belief held steady even in the midst of sensual splendor, of one whose deliberate caution served her well in time of trouble, of one whose unfeigned modesty attested to a disciplined spirit. Esther's life was one of consistent commitment and pure conscience, one of divine dependence and self-control.

Born in 1867, William Pierson Merrill was a minister of rare insight, one whose pulpits included Philadelphia, Chicago, and New York. But today, Merrill is best remembered not for his eloquent sermons, but rather for his hymn "Rise Up, O Men of God."

It was while crossing Lake Michigan aboard a steamer, on his way to fill a Sunday appointment in his Chicago pulpit, that Mr. Merrill began to meditate on his own ministry in the light of that of Jesus. As he mentally reviewed the Gospels, he became impressed with Christ's words to the impotent man at the pool of Bethesda (John 5:8), to the paralytic (Luke 5:23), and to the man with the withered hand (Luke 6:8). In each case, Christ's healing had begun with the same command, "Rise up!"

With those two words as his starting point of inspiration, William Pierson Merrill wrote his stirring hymn.

Rise up, O men of God!
Have done with lesser things;
Give heart and mind and soul and strength
To serve the Kings of Kings.

Rise up, O men of God!
His kingdom tarries long;
Bring in the day of brotherhood
And end the night of wrong.

Rise up, O men of God!
The Church for you doth wait,
Her strength unequal to her task;
Rise up and make her great!

Lift high the cross of Christ!
Tread where His feet have trod.
As brothers of the Son of Man,
Rise up, O men of God!

The call today is for self-controlled Christians, who will "have done with lesser things" of this world, for Spirit-filled men and women who will give themselves selflessly to the work of God's kingdom.

---

In final preparation for my teaching degree, I student-taught at the high school level. After I had been in the building for several weeks, a reporter from the high school newspaper came to do an interview with me. After all the usual questions about my education, family, and hobbies, he asked me, "What do you think a teacher's most important job is?" I became so excited! I knew the answer to that question—thanks to my general education professor. Early in the semester, she had given us a fifty-two word sentence explaining what the real task of a teacher is. We then had to memorize that sentence and write it on the back of every exam we took in her class. So I gave that sixteen-year-old reporter my biggest smile, took a deep breath, and launched into my answer: "Basically, the task of the teacher is to provide a set of experiences which will bring about a progressive series of changes, characterized by orderliness and coherent design, leading to a desired functional operation of the human organism and which will both facilitate and supplement the natural development of the human organism."

That poor reporter was so awed by my response that he stared for a moment at his blank paper before turning to my critic teacher, who had been teaching for twenty-three years and was head of the English department. He posed the same question to her. I imagine he thought if someone of my tender age could spout such wisdom, what would this veteran teacher say? Without a moment's hesitation, she quipped, "A teacher's job is to force abstract ideas into concrete heads!"

Titus 2:11-14 says:

> For the grace of God that brings salvation has appeared to all men. It teaches us to say "No" to ungodliness and worldly passions, and to live self-controlled, upright and godly lives in this present age, while we wait for the blessed hope—the glorious appearing of our great God and Savior, Jesus Christ, who gave himself for us to redeem us from all wickedness and to purify for himself a people that are his very own, eager to do what is good.

It is grace that teaches us the abstract and difficult things of the Spirit, things like discipline and self-control. It is this unmerited favor of God, completely and consistently applied to our lives, that forces into our "concrete" heads both the necessity of holy living and the availability of divine strength. When we pledge ourselves to life in the Spirit, we are not given a creed to memorize; we are given a challenge to meet—the challenge of learning to say NO! to fleshly desires and indulgences. We become students of holiness, taught by grace, tutored and transformed by the Holy Spirit's presence in our lives.

Self-control. It's not just a virtue you slip on when you decide to tame your temper tantrums or need to lose ten pounds. It's an element essential in daily Christian living. Every self must know the surrender of passion before it can know the power of temperance—yourself, myself. "The fruit of the Spirit is . . . self-control."

# CONCLUSION

*Sow for yourselves righteousness,*
  *reap the fruit of unfailing love,*
*and break up your unplowed ground;*
  *for it is time to seek the Lord,*
*until he comes*
  *and showers righteousness on you.*

Hosea 10:12

*H*ER NAME WAS JUNIPER, AND SHE HAD THE MOST comfortable back in the world.

We were both five years old that spring, and Juniper had just been broken to the plow. While my father tilled our garden plot, I rode on Juniper's wide, white back. I watched as the hard ground broke open under the blade of our turning plow. Soon both my father and Juniper were soaked with sweat. It had been no easy task, but together they had transformed our garden into soft, black dirt. Now it could accept the seeds of sweet corn and cucumbers and watermelons.

For the next few weeks, Juniper and I kept watch over that garden spot. Together we would look through the rough slats of the gate. And as her velvet nose nuzzled my arm, I talked to her, repeating what all the grown-ups kept telling me. "Soon this place will be bustin' with good things to eat!" Of course, in due time, it was—perfectly striped melons, corn so sweet it didn't even need butter, beans and carrots and huge red beets.

Preparation is an essential element in any harvest. We, as Christians, must be diligent in preparing our hearts for seeds of righteousness. We must break up clods of sin and self; we must plow the stubborn ground of our hearts; we must patiently tend the tender shoot of salvation. It's not easy, but it is imperative. Only then can we reap a "bumper crop" of the fruit of the Spirit: love, joy, peace, patience, kindness, goodness, faithfulness, gentleness, and self-control.

Even now the Holy Spirit waits to seed your heart, to plant in you the potential for abundant fruit.

Why not let him?